SPEAK LORD

I'M LISTENING

*How to Hear God's Voice
Above the Noise*

Larry Kreider

Regal

From Gospel Light
Ventura, California, U.S.A.

Published by Regal
From Gospel Light
Ventura, California, U.S.A.
www.regalbooks.com
Printed in the U.S.A.

Library of Congress Cataloging-in-Publication Data
Kreider, Larry.
Speak, Lord, I'm listening : how to hear God's voice above the noise / Larry Kreider.
p. cm.
ISBN 978-0-8307-4612-5 (trade paper)
1. Spirituality. 2. Spiritual life—Christianity. 3. Listening—Religious aspects—Christianity. 4. Discernment (Christian theology) I. Title.
BV4501.3.K74 2008
248.4—dc22
2008008881

Rights for publishing this book outside the U.S.A. or in non-English languages are administered by Gospel Light Worldwide, an international not-for-profit ministry. For additional information, please visit www.glww.org, email info@glww.org, or write to Gospel Light Worldwide, 1957 Eastman Avenue, Ventura, CA 93003, U.S.A.

This book is dedicated to my amazing wife, LaVerne,
the love of my life and my partner in ministry;
to our four wonderful children, Katrina, Charita, Joshua and Leticia,
along with our son-in-law, David,
who is such a blessing to us;
and to our very special grandchildren,
Connor, Jocelyn and Ella, who have brought us great joy.

Speak, Lord . . . I am listening.

1 SAMUEL 3:9, *NCV*

Contents

V. Wisdom, Counsel and the Church

VI. Spiritual Disciplines and Taking Action

VII. Discernment and Spiritual Warfare

VIII. Divine Encounters

Epilogue 230
Learning to Listen

Author Contact 233

Acknowledgments

A very special thanks goes to Karen Ruiz, my writing assistant and editor, who does a superb job. Another thank-you to those who gave valuable insight to the book: Peter Bunton, Katrina Brechbill, Jessi Clemmer, JoAnn Kunz, Diane Omondi, Steve Prokopchak, Brian Sauder, Sarah Sauder, and many others too numerous to mention. We love and appreciate all of you.

Tuning In to God

Much of this book was written on airplanes and in places like Kenya, Brazil and India. Nearly every weekend I find myself traveling to one of the U.S. states or to another country to teach from the Bible. For a long time, I was under the impression that the way I learned to recognize God's voice (based on my background and culture) was the same way that everyone else hears Him. Then one day it dawned on me that people in different cultures, both here and abroad, learn to hear the voice of God in so many different ways.

Since that day, I have been on a personal journey to identify and compile the many ways that God speaks to His people. Not surprisingly, I came to realize that I had been somewhat narrow-minded in how I thought the Lord could speak to me. I had missed hearing His voice so many times. He had been speaking to me over and over again, and I didn't even realize it! It was similar to young Samuel in the Bible, who heard someone speaking but didn't recognize that it was God. Samuel had not yet learned to recognize the voice of his heavenly Father (see 1 Sam. 3:7).

God's Voice Stands Out Above the Noise

More than 40 years ago, I heard a voice that compelled my attention. I was at a friend's house when I heard the muffled voices of a group of girls having a party upstairs. Among the muted sounds of the girls' laughter and talk, I kept hearing a recurring voice that captured my attention. "Whose voice is that?" I inquired of a friend. He knew the voice, because it was a friend of his—LaVerne. But it was the first time I had heard her voice, and I was intrigued. In fact, I was so intrigued that I married her seven years later, and now I know her voice anywhere.

Jesus told His disciples that sheep follow the shepherd "because they know his voice" (John 10:4). How did they know his voice? They had learned from experience to trust the voice of their shepherd.

To hear God's voice clearly, we must have a growing love relationship with God and trust Him. It's that simple. The more intimately we know God, the more immediate will be our recognition of His voice through all the noise of life.

The Bible is filled with examples of ordinary people who heard the voice of a mighty God speaking to them. In the book of Genesis, we read that Adam and Eve walked and talked with God in the Garden of Eden (see Gen. 3:8). The Lord startled Moses at a flaming bush in the desert when He called Moses to deliver the Israelites from the bondage of slavery in Egypt (see Exod. 3:2-3). God advised Joshua to be strong and courageous (see Josh. 1:9), and gave David fresh strategies for each battle against his enemies (see 1 Chron. 11-21). The Lord told Mary that she would be the mother of Jesus (see Luke 1:26-33). God affirmed Jesus at His baptism through a voice from heaven (see Luke 3:21-22). Paul was thoroughly transformed by the Lord's voice on the Damascus Road (see Acts 9).

God delights in revealing Himself to us. He promises to answer if we call on Him. "Call to me and I will answer you and tell you great and unsearchable things you do not know" (Jer. 33:3). When we pray, we engage in conversation with God, and God responds.

God has heard and answered my call many times. When I was 11, He spoke to me about my need for Jesus, and that's when I first gave my life to Christ. When I was 18, He showed me that I was a hypocrite, causing me to repent and submit to His Lordship. When I was a young adult, the Lord spoke to me and my fiancée (LaVerne) to get married and become missionaries. We obeyed.

In 1980, the Lord spoke to me about starting a new kind of church built through small groups. LaVerne and I gathered a few others together and started a new church that eventually grew into a worldwide church movement.

These are only a few major highlights of hearing God's voice. God has made Himself known to me countless times over the years. He has spoken to me on thousands of occasions, in a variety of ways.

Sometimes I have found it difficult to hear His voice clearly. Many times I thought I had heard the Lord's voice only to find that I had not. At other times, I felt like I was tuning a radio to a specific frequency—but I had to ignore the mass of static and strange voices coming in to zero in on the one voice for which I was searching. There are often so many thoughts running through my mind. What is, and is not, His voice?

After 40 years of learning to listen to God's voice, I have found that He is always speaking, but we're not always listening. If you want to learn more about how to distinguish God's voice, I invite you on a journey with me as I share what I have learned about the many ways He speaks to us, including the ways that we often miss. There is nothing more important than learning to hear God's voice, because one word from Him will change your life forever!

Selective Hearing?

Even Jesus' disciples did not always hear Him correctly or recognize His voice. When Jesus joined two of His disciples on the road to Emmaus after His resurrection from the dead, and He began talking to them, they didn't recognize Him even though they had walked, talked and eaten meals with Him for the past three years (see Luke 24:13-32). Perhaps they were so immersed in the details of the dark events of the past few days that they couldn't hear clearly.

I imagine there was a good chance they did not see Jesus because they simply did not expect to see Him. He appeared to them in an unfamiliar form, at an unexpected time, and their ears and eyes remained closed.

Before we criticize these disciples, we must ask ourselves, "How often do we experience the same loss of hearing today?" Could it be that the Lord sometimes speaks to us in ways that are unfamiliar to us, and we don't recognize His voice? We lament that we can't hear Him speak, but in reality He has been speaking all along. Could it be that our understanding of hearing His voice is limited? Maybe we have preconceived ideas of how God will or will not communicate with us, and they limit us in hearing His voice.

I'm convinced that we should not get too selective about the method in which the Lord speaks to us. Instead, we need to stay open to His speaking to us in any way He chooses. I spend much of my time traveling throughout the world, teaching the Bible. One of the things I miss most when I travel is being with my family. I really miss spending time with my wife, LaVerne. However, because of the technologically advanced age in which we live, I can usually communicate with her regardless of where I am in the world. I don't care whether the message comes by phone, fax, email, letter, or note, I just want to hear from her.

In the same way, God desires to build a relationship with us, which happens primarily by having ongoing dialogue with Him—talking and listening. From the very beginning of time, God desired a two-way communication between Himself and mankind. Adam and Eve were tuned to God as they "heard the sound of the Lord God as he was walking in the garden in the cool of the day" (Gen. 3:8).

This is how God wants to relate to us as well. It is God's desire to walk and communicate with His children. He longs for you to hear His loving, distinct voice.

In this book, we will explore how the Lord speaks to us. I have discovered more than 50 ways, and I've grouped them in 8 general life settings. In the first chapter, for example, we will start with the first and foremost way of hearing God speak—through His written word, the Bible. This is the purest and surest way that God speaks to us. Jesus said, "If you hold to my teaching, you are really my disciples. Then you will know the truth, and the truth will set you free" (John 8:31-32). We will never go off track if we obey the Word of God.

Throughout the coming chapters, let's seek God together and discover the many ways in which we have already experienced His voice, and then learn about the many ways we have yet to hear Him above all the noise of life. He is speaking, and He is waiting for us to hear.

Section One

READING, WRITING AND MEDITATION

1

The Bible

One evening, after putting his children to bed, my friend Jimmy was heading for the TV, but for some reason he picked up his Bible instead and began to read. He opened the Scriptures and read his psalm for the day. When he got to verse 5 of Psalm 30, "weeping may remain for a night, but rejoicing comes in the morning," he felt a very gentle touch telling him that something very horrible was about to happen, but it would end with joy, and he was not to fear. Jimmy immediately told his wife, Deb, what he sensed and then went to bed wondering what could possibly be so bad.

The next day, Jimmy and Deb had to take their three-year-old daughter Nicole to the hospital. She was complaining that her legs and back were sore and said she could not walk. Within an hour, she was diagnosed with cancer. She was immediately brought to the cancer ward and started on chemotherapy. Over the next couple of days, they learned that the chemo was not working, and Nicole was in serious trouble. They brought in the elders from their church to pray. Within a couple of days, the condition reversed and the chemo did its work.

Though three other children in the hospital died, Nicole was back at home within a couple of weeks. Over the next three years, Nicole endured various chemo treatments and faced many obstacles. But with every cancer-free year, her prognosis was increasingly more hopeful.

Today, at 23 years of age, Nicole is a beautiful young woman living a very abundant life. Jimmy told me, "It was that word from Scripture that kept us through many hard years of chemo treatments as we watched our little girl endure so much pain. The Lord's promise from His Word spoke to us and sustained us during this difficult time."

The Bible is God's personal love letter to you. From it, He speaks to you, directs you and molds you for His purposes and plans. In every generation, the Bible has been viewed as a source to understand the world we live in and the reason for our existence. Christians read it with the expectation that God will speak through its words. The Bible must be the first and last word in your life; it is your ultimate authority, the gauge with which to measure the direction of your life. In the Greek, there are two words that describe God's Word—*logos* and *rhema*. *Logos* is the truth revealed (established), and *rhema* is the truth speaking and communicating personally (illuminating our lives). The *rhema* word of the Lord is the "voice" of the tried-and-proven, established Word of God. The *rhema* word is made alive, as though God has just spoken it into your ears. His *rhema* word will always be supported in the established truth revealed in the *logos* Word of God. The *logos* word confirms whether or not what you think is the *rhema* word of the Lord really is His voice.

God can take the *logos* word and make it *rhema* to you personally. Sometimes a Scripture will seem to jump out at you—it comes alive in a particular way for you. That is when the *logos* becomes a specific *rhema* to you. It becomes alive when you apply it to your life. The Bible would be a lifeless history book without this kind of personal revelation.

As a new believer, I had often read the verse from John 10:10: "I came that they might have life, and might have it abundantly" (*NASB*). I knew this verse of Scripture to be true (*logos*); but one day it became *rhema* to me. I realized that God actually wanted me to experience His abundance in my life! My outlook changed from that day on.

Another time, I felt completely overwhelmed with life. I felt overloaded and fatigued with my job, the ministry I was involved in, family financial struggles. I remember jumping into my car in response to a call from a friend who needed a ride, and on the way, I felt completely despondent. Then Scripture came to my mind—a verse I had memorized a few months before: "I have been crucified with Christ and I no longer live, but Christ lives in me" (Gal. 2:20). The words "Christ lives in me" literally stimulated me. I realized that Jesus Christ actually lives inside of me! Within a few minutes, my entire disposition began to change. I regained strength to go on. I felt like a whole new person. God's Word came alive in me. *God spoke to me through His Word.*

Correctly Interpreting the Bible for Your Life

God's Word never changes. Many times, however, the area in which you need guidance is not specifically addressed in Scripture. You may need to know the answers for some of the following questions: *What is the Lord's plan for my career? Whom should I marry? Do I need to consider further training? Where should I live? Should I buy a house or rent a house? Should I go to college? With which group of believers has the Lord called me to serve?* This is the time to learn to listen to the voice of the Holy Spirit speaking to your spirit, and confirm it by His written Word.

It is extremely important to correctly interpret the original intent of what you read in the Bible so that you can apply God's Word intelligently to your situation. When you read, listen to the voice of God coming through His Word, and avoid taking Scripture out of context or misusing it for your own interpretation. The Bible never contradicts itself, but sometimes it can be taken out of context. For example, if you take no regard for context, Paul seems to contradict himself by saying at one place that we are not saved by works (see Eph. 2:8-9) and in another place that we're to work out our salvation (see Phil. 2:12). Scripture, read in context, will reconcile these two seemingly opposing Scripture passages.

If some Scripture passages are hard to understand, do your homework and study the meaning and context of the passage. Because our modern culture is different from that of Bible times, we often have a cultural gap that needs to be interpreted. You can ask a seasoned believer who has studied hermeneutics (the principles of biblical interpretation) to help you understand what the Lord is saying through a Scripture that doesn't make sense to you. For the Old Testament, use a Hebrew dictionary to look up the use of certain words. For the New Testament, use a Greek dictionary to do the same.

Feed on the Bible

If you want to hear God's voice, you must study the Bible. Of all the other ways that God may speak to you, He will never contradict His written word. When Jesus was tempted by the devil, He made it clear that God's Word is what gives us life and strength. "Man does not live on bread alone, but on every word that comes from the mouth of God" (Matt. 4:4). The Bible contains the food your soul requires. You must feed on God's written word for spiritual health. You do that by saturating your mind with the Word of God. You can read through it a few chapters at a time or meditate on a particular section of the Bible, such as the four Gospels or the epistles. You may want to read through the book of Psalms for months at a time. Many people read one chapter of

Proverbs a day for a month, because there are 31 chapters.

Memorizing God's Word allows you to "hide" it in your heart. Sometimes you will want to read and reread one verse over and over and meditate on it.

Jesus reveals that the words He has spoken to us are spirit and life (see John 6:63). God's Word divides between truth and deception (see Heb. 4:12). If God has truly spoken to you, it will always line up with the Bible. You must have a full reservoir of the Word of God to draw from so that the Enemy can't deceive you. Any dream, prophecy, vision or audible voice that does not line up with God's written Word is not the voice of God. Scripture is given as a standard so that you will never get off track. God's Word is described this way: "All Scripture is God-breathed and is useful for teaching, rebuking, correcting and training in righteousness, so that the man of God may be thoroughly equipped for every good work" (2 Tim. 3:16-17).

The Bible is your final authority: "Study and be eager and do your utmost to present yourself to God approved, a workman who has no cause to be ashamed, correctly analyzing and accurately dividing the Word of Truth" (2 Tim. 2:15, *AMP*). The Bible gives you direct guidance on many issues of life. For example, the Bible tells us that it is a sin to commit sexual immorality (see Eph. 5:3). If you do not know what the Bible says, you can be easily deceived into thinking that whatever you are feeling is the Lord leading you. This is very dangerous. That's why you must study the Scriptures.

The Bible Is a Plumb Line for Revelation

If anyone claims to have supernatural revelation from God, it must agree with His Word (see 1 Cor. 14:37). Paul the apostle urges the Galatian believers not to be persuaded by false teachers:

> I am astonished that you are so quickly deserting the one who called you by the grace of Christ and are turning to a different gospel—which is really no gospel at all. Evidently some people are throwing you into confusion and are trying to pervert the gospel of Christ. But even if we or an angel from heaven should preach a gospel other than the one we preached to you, let him be eternally condemned! (Gal. 1:6-8).

Just because someone quotes Scripture does not mean they necessarily have God's intentions in mind.

Remember, the Bible says that Satan comes to us like an angel of light (see 2 Cor. 11:14). In order not to be deceived, we should be like the Bereans who checked whether the Christian interpretation Paul put on the Old Testament Scriptures was the true one (see Acts 17:10-12). They checked everything by the written Word of God, and we should too. The written Word of God is our standard to be sure that the revelation we are receiving is in line with the perfect will of God. We know that the Holy Spirit gave the words to the writers of the Scriptures, so He will not speak anything to us that disagrees with the Scriptures.

Reading the Bible is an essential way to hear God's voice. It is certainly an accurate method and one in which you and I need to be hearing from our heavenly Father on a daily basis. The more you read God's Word, the more you will love it, and the more you will hear His voice speak personally and directly to you. He loves you, and He wants to speak with you.

Apply What You've Learned

VERSE TO REMEMBER:

The words I have spoken to you are spirit and they are life.
JOHN 6:63

1. How is the Bible a measuring stick to gauge your life?

2. Explain the difference between God's *rhema* word and *logos* word.

3. How have you personally heard God speak to you through the Bible?

A Journal

Although God had brought significant freedom to her life, Nicki, a new Christian, still dealt with considerable emotional pain from past experiences. The Lord prompted her to begin a "journal of healing" that involved writing down passages of Scripture that "jumped off the page into her spirit" or God-inspired thoughts that people spoke to her. She also wrote down nuggets of truth from Christian literature. Recording in her journal what God was speaking to her in these various ways helped Nicki gain clarity about hearing His voice and also helped her find healing and wholeness.

A journal is a written record of your thoughts recorded on paper or computer. When you keep a journal, you simply transcribe what is in your heart—your thoughts, prayers, fears, disappointments, joys, impressions. Keeping a journal allows you to record your sequence of thoughts and then go back to them later. It is often surprising how much clearer things can become when you prayerfully explore your thoughts at a later date.

Some people love to keep a journal, and others think of it as a chore. Whether you write for a specific period of time or for a particular reason, writing down your thoughts in a journal is another way to hear God speaking to you.

Did you know that the Bible tells us that God keeps a journal? Malachi 3:16 says that those who love the Lord talked together, and God listened and then He placed their words in a scroll of remembrance!

What Goes into a Journal

Sometimes you may record a Scripture that God makes alive to your heart and mind. You may have read the verse a hundred times, but this time it really grabs you. That's because God is speaking to you! Record it in your journal for when you need it most. Proverbs says, "Store up my commandments within you. . . . Write them on the tablet of your heart" (Prov. 7:1,3).

I've heard someone say that the only thing required of writing in a journal is honesty. Keeping a journal is like keeping a spiritual diary. Writing down your honest thoughts and God's responses to your requests, thoughts, feelings and insights provides a way of remembering God's activity in your life. A journal helps you look back over a period of time—months, or even years—and see a written record of the Lord's dealings in your life.

When the prophet Habakkuk needed an answer from the Lord, the Lord replied by mentioning the importance of writing down what He said to him and waiting for a reply.

> I will stand at my watch and station myself on the ramparts; I will look to see what he will say to me, and what answer I am to give to this complaint. Then the Lord replied: "Write down the revelation and make it plain on tablets so that a herald may run with it. For the revelation awaits an appointed time; it speaks of the end and will not prove false. Though it linger, wait for it; it will certainly come and will not delay" (Hab. 2:1-3).

Habakkuk was a prophet who sought to hear God speak. First he went to a quiet place where he would be alone, and waited to hear from God. He listened and looked to hear what God would say. When God began to speak, He told Habakkuk to record the vision that he was sensing in his heart. God clearly showed His prophet how to dialogue with Him by using the combination of coming to a quiet place, listening and journaling.

Write It Down to Preserve It!

Writing what God is speaking to you becomes a reminder of the revelation God has given to you that has not yet come to pass. When the Lord speaks to me, I write it down so that I don't lose it. There are things that God spoke to me more than 20 years ago that are only now coming to pass. Those revelations often look much different from what I expected. If I had not written them down, I would no longer have them to help guide me into what God has for me today.

Writing in a journal is one method to help you learn to discern God's voice better. In *How to Hear God's Voice*, Mark and Patti Virkler state that one of the greatest benefits of using a journal during time spent with the Lord is that it allows you "to receive freely the spontaneous flow of ideas that come to your mind in faith, believing that they are from Jesus, without short-circuiting them by subjecting them to rational and sensory doubt."[1] They further explain it like this:

> I found that before I began keeping a journal, I would ask God for an answer to a question, and as soon as an idea came into my mind, I would immediately question whether the idea was from God or from self; and, in so doing, I was short-circuiting the intuitive flow of the Spirit by subjecting it to rational doubt. . . . I would receive one idea from God and doubt that it was from Him, and therefore receive no more. Now, by writing it down, I can receive whole pages in faith, knowing I will have ample time to test it later. . . . Maintaining a journal keeps your mind occupied (therefore, out of the way) and on track as you are receiving God's words.[2]

Some people object to writing in a journal because they compare it to Satan's counterpart—automatic writing. Journaling is not to be confused with demonically inspired automatic writing, which allows you to be overtaken by a demonic spirit that controls your hand to write down what a voice is telling you. Instead, biblical journaling comes from the flow of ideas birthed by God in your heart and then writing those thoughts down with your hand under your own control. These spontaneous thoughts, feelings and impressions should always be tested and examined later to be sure they line up with Scripture.

God's Words to You in Black and White

Journaling is really just a written record of how God has been working in your life. God may speak to you today about something that you need 10 years down the road. Journal records let you look back over the years and see how God has been faithful to hear and answer your prayers, and discover how you have grown spiritually. It is a way of holding yourself accountable to move on to spiritual maturity.

Journaling can also be a form of meditative worship. When you are alone with God, you can explore your passion for the Lord as you write to your Father what is on your heart.

You can use a simple spiral-bound notebook or a fancier hardbound journal to keep track of your impressions, inspired thoughts and Scriptures. Your journal could even be your computer. I have heard of some who use tape recorders to record the thoughts coming to them during their time with God. I have a friend who calls his voice mail on his cell phone in order to record what he has heard. At a later time, he writes those thoughts in his journal. Any of these methods of keeping track of hearing from God are viable.

Twenty-five years ago, during a personal time with God, I felt an impression from the Lord that a man from Japan was coming to help me. I wrote this in my journal. Nearly every day for many years, I asked God for a "man from Japan" to come into my life. More than 10 years later, I was sitting in a restaurant with a new friend from Colorado, who leaned across the table and told me, "I am that man." His ancestry was Japanese, and he has become a close friend who has helped me numerous times in strategic ways during the past 15 years. I am so glad I wrote this impression in my journal, or I might have forgotten it and never experienced the fulfillment of this insight from God.

Cultivating an ever-deepening relationship with the Lord through journaling helps us focus the eyes of our heart on God and receive fresh words from Him each day.

Apply What You've Learned

VERSE TO REMEMBER:

Write down the revelation and make it plain on tablets. . . . For the revelation awaits an appointed time; it speaks of the end and will not prove false. Though it linger, wait for it; it will certainly come and will not delay.
HABAKKUK 2:2-3

1. How do you think journaling can help you hear from God?

2. Why is it important to "test" what you write in your journal?

3. If you do not already keep a journal to record God's activity in your life, try it for a specific period of time. At the end of that time, summarize what you've heard from God. Discuss any answers to prayer that you received.

Notes
1. Mark and Patti Virkler, *How to Hear God's Voice* (Shippensburg, PA: Destiny Image, 2005), p. 120.
2. Ibid.

3

Meditation and Contemplation

"It's not that prayer isn't enough," Jim told me, "but when I meditate, I have a God-given longing for Him that is fulfilled, and I know that it is God, and God alone, who is sufficient."

Jim continued to describe to me how his relationship with the Lord had been revitalized by meditation and contemplation: "Meditation moves me beyond the words of prayer to a contemplative aspect of being consumed in God's love as I focus on what He has to say to me through His Word. I experience His nearness in ways that are almost indescribable."

Somebody once said that the mind is like a tree full of monkeys jumping from branch to branch. The whirl of distractions that clamor for our attention when we try to quiet ourselves often involve the usual cast of characters—our "to do" list, a chore we should have done yesterday—the list could go on. Sometimes it seems virtually impossible to slow down enough to quiet our mind so that we can focus on what God is saying to us.

In the Old Testament, there are two primary Hebrew words for meditation: *haga*, which means "to utter, groan, meditate" or "ponder"; and *sihach*, which means "to muse, rehearse in one's mind or contemplate." Meditation involves a deliberate action on the part of the individual to ponder or think.

Author Bill Johnson says that if we've ever worried about something, we already know how to meditate, because every person meditates every day.

> The question is, what are you meditating on? . . . We must get our minds set on spiritual things because as long as we fill our minds with what's happening in the natural, we restrict our effectiveness. . . . The solution? To meditate on the Word and give ourselves every opportunity to remember what is true.[1]

I like the way Rick Warren, in *The Purpose Driven Life*, describes meditation on the Word of God:

Meditation is focused thinking. It takes serious effort. You
select a verse and reflect on it over and over in your mind. . . .
No other habit can do more to transform your life and make
you more like Jesus than daily reflection on Scripture.[2]

The early monks read the Bible slowly as they carefully considered the deep meaning of Scripture. Meditation occurred as they pon-
dered a specific topic and immersed themselves in it. Often they found
themselves praying spontaneously as a result of this intense meditation and focus on God's Word; you could say it moved them into a
more intimate experience with God, or a contemplative state.

What Sets Christian Meditation Apart

Western Christians today are often a bit leery of meditation because it
is generally seen as a practice of the New Age movement and its asso-
ciation with Transcendental Meditation (TM), which is steeped in
Hindu philosophy. There are two major differences, however, between
other forms of meditation and Christian meditation. In Christian
meditation, the believer seeks to fill his or her thoughts with truths
about God from the Word of God. "But his delight is in the law of the
LORD, and on his law he meditates day and night" (Ps. 1:2). Rather
than emptying oneself, the Christian fills his or her mind with the
promises that God has given in His Word.

In meditation that is practiced with some yoga techniques or by
Hindu gurus and Buddhist monks, the individual seeks to empty self
or consciousness of all thoughts, often using a tool called a mantra—
a word or sounds that the person repeats until the mind is completely
empty. This exercise is supposed to allow relaxation and a relief from
stress. However, in this disconnection between the body and spirit, or
altered state of consciousness, a doorway to a false spirit can be
opened to the human soul. In sharp contrast, God's Word encourages
us to fill our minds with (meditate on) the Word of God. As we do so,
the Holy Spirit illuminates the Word of God from our spirit to our
minds, and we are changed.

You could simplify the differences between Christian meditation
and other meditation by saying that Christian meditation dwells on
the already revealed or inspired revelation of God's Word, and God as

the object of worship and adoration; other forms of meditation seek some new truth to be revealed, with the object of worship being self.

Meditate on God's Word

To grow spiritually and hear God's voice more clearly, we must meditate on the Word of God each day. In this way, our spirit receives God's Word, and the Holy Spirit begins the process of mind renewal. If we don't fill our minds with the truth of God's Word, we can get sidetracked by the world's philosophies. Exercising faith in God involves reading God's Word and obeying it.

How do you meditate on the Word of God? To meditate simply means to roll something around over and over again in your mind. Joshua 1:8 tells us, "Do not let this Book of the Law depart from your mouth; meditate on it day and night, so that you may be careful to do everything written in it. Then you will be prosperous and successful."

An example from agricultural life provides a picture of the meditation process. Cows have multiple stomachs. After they fill up with hay or grass, they spend the rest of the day laying under a shade tree "chewing their cud." Food is passed from one stomach to the other in stages as they intermittently regurgitate it and chew it again. We could liken this process to meditating on the Word of God. We need to read the Word, ponder it, write portions of it down and bring it to mind numerous times throughout the day to memorize it and meditate on it spiritually (to chew on it!).

When I gave my life to Christ, every day I wrote down on an index card a verse of Scripture that seemed to have special significance to me. Throughout the day, I pulled out the card to memorize it and meditate on its meaning. I literally "rolled around" God's Word in my mind until it became a part of me. During my first few years as a new Christian, I memorized hundreds of verses of Scripture this way.

We are to meditate on the Lord Himself (see Ps. 63:6), His wonderful works (see Ps. 77:12) and His revealed word (see Ps. 119:15,23,48,97-98,148). According to the apostle Paul, we are to meditate on "whatever is true, whatever is noble, whatever is right, whatever is pure, whatever is lovely, whatever is admirable—if anything is excellent or praiseworthy—think about such things" (Phil. 4:8).

The purpose of meditation, then, is to allow God to nourish us with His revealed will so that we receive spiritual joy and strength and are blessed. "Blessed is the man, [whose] delight is in the law of the LORD, and on his law he meditates day and night" (Ps. 1:2).

The Bible has some powerful things to say about spiritual meditation. For example, Psalm 1:2 says that we need to make God's Word our primary focus for meditation and reminds us to read it contemplatively every day. We should not only read His Word silently, but occasionally read it aloud to ourselves. The Hebrew word for "meditate" here means "to mutter." As we read slowly and audibly, we can focus our mind on the words and their meaning.

In Psalm 19:14, we find David praying, "May the words of my mouth and the meditation of my heart be pleasing in your sight, O LORD, my Rock and my Redeemer."

When we meditate on God's Word, says Jan Johnson, "We savor the text and enter into it. . . . We read to let God speak to us in light of the facts already absorbed. Meditation, then, builds the skill of hearing God at the heart and soul level."[3] Meditation is holding the Word of God in our heart until it has affected every part of our life.

Apply What You've Learned

VERSE TO REMEMBER:

Blessed is the man . . . [whose] delight is in the law of the Lord,
and on his law he meditates day and night.
PSALM 1:1-2

1. On what do you meditate? On what do you ponder?

2. Have you ever felt yourself moved beyond the words of prayer to a contemplative aspect of being consumed in God's love and presence? Describe it.

3. How do you meditate on God's Word? Give an example of how He has spoken to you during these times.

Notes
1. Bill Johnson, *The Supernatural Power of a Transformed Mind* (Shippensburg, PA: Destiny Image Publishers, Inc., 2005), p. 114.
2. Rick Warren, *The Purpose Driven Life* (Grand Rapids, MI: Zondervan, 2002), p. 190.
3. Jan Johnson, *Savoring God's Word* (Colorado Springs, CO: NavPress, 2004), p. 4.

Section Two

PRAYER, PRAISE AND WORSHIP

4

Praise and Thanksgiving

God is a relational God. He just loves to hang out with you! When you take time to sincerely seek God, I believe that His heart is wide open to hearing all that you have to say, and He freely responds.

To praise God means to respond to God for who He is and for what He has done. When you thank God for specific things He has done in your life, and for who He is, you open yourself up to hearing from Him. Living a life of praise and thanksgiving releases the presence of God in our lives.

St. Augustine of Hippo (A.D. 354-430) is quoted as having said, "He who sings, prays twice." When we sing and praise God from the heart, something happens. Our song and posture of praise help us see and understand God in a deeper way! We take our eyes off of our circumstances and put them on the Creator of all things. We place ourselves in a position to hear from Him.

The Password to His Presence

The Bible says that God inhabits the praises of His people (see Ps. 22:3). God "lives" in the atmosphere of His praise. Said another way, praise brings us into the presence and power of God. Praise (and thanksgiving) is the "password" that allows us to come before Him.

In the Old Testament, God literally came into the Temple while the singers worshiped God:

> The trumpeters and singers joined in unison, as with one voice, to give praise and thanks to the Lord. Accompanied by trumpets, cymbals and other instruments, they raised their voices in praise to the LORD and sang: "He is good; his love endures forever." Then the temple of the LORD was filled with a cloud, and the priests could not perform their service because of the cloud, for the glory of the LORD filled the temple of God (2 Chron. 5:13-14).

The whole spiritual environment was changed when God was praised. Our spiritual environment can change when we offer God our praise and thanksgiving. For example, do you often feel stressed out? God says that His peace far surpasses all our ideas of how we can resolve our anxieties, and we acquire that peace by talking to Him and walking with Him in a constant attitude of thanksgiving. Philippians 4:6 tells us that we should "not be anxious about anything, but in everything, by prayer and petition, with thanksgiving, present your requests to God."

When we lay our lives before the Lord and thank Him and praise Him for who He is and for what He has done, His peace will stand guard at the door of our hearts and minds, and change us.

> And the peace of God, which transcends all understanding, will guard your hearts and your minds in Christ Jesus. Finally, brothers, whatever is true, whatever is noble, whatever is right, whatever is pure, whatever is lovely, whatever is admirable—if anything is excellent or praiseworthy—think about such things (Phil. 4:7-8).

Choosing to praise and thank the Lord for His goodness and grace opens the door wide for us to experience His presence in our lives each day.

Praise Is a Sacrifice

I must confess, I don't always feel like praising God; but praising the Lord is not dependent upon my emotions; it is a decision I make.

As you come to the Lord each day, you are really offering Him a sacrifice of praise. "Through Jesus, therefore, let us continually offer to God a sacrifice of praise—the fruit of lips that confess his name" (Heb. 13:15). With your sacrifice of praise, you establish intimacy with Him. You are saying that you believe in Him and want to please Him. You are telling God that you believe He is in control of your circumstances (see Rom. 8:28).

Offering a sacrifice of praise means talking to yourself as you talk to God. The Bible says that David talked to himself; he "encouraged himself in the Lord" (1 Sam. 30:6, *KJV*). Another time, we see David telling his soul to give praise to the Lord: "Praise the Lord, O my soul; and all my inmost being, praise his holy name!" (Ps. 103:1). Each day you can tell your soul to give praise to the Lord who knows how to encourage you.

Praise Lifts

Offering praise and thanksgiving to God helps crowd out those things in our life that hold us back, such as criticism, depression and fear. If we have a critical spirit toward others or toward the circumstances in our life, we sabotage our peace. The prayer of praise is our greatest weapon against a critical spirit. Isaiah records, "You will keep in perfect peace all who trust in you, all whose thoughts are fixed on you!" (Isa. 26:3, *NLT*). By praising and thanking Him daily, we show trust in the Lord and leave no room for criticism to weigh us down.

Many people today struggle with depression, but it is not a new problem. Even the psalmist was downcast and could not understand why. "Why am I discouraged? Why is my heart so sad?" (Ps. 42:5, *NLT*). As believers, we know that depression is not a condition we want to be in, but we find ourselves there and brood over why we feel this way. The psalmist finally decides to stop asking why and instead chooses to praise the Lord in spite of his depression. "I will put my hope in God! I will praise him again—my Savior and my God" (Ps. 42:5-6, *NLT*). When we praise the Lord even in discouraging times, we are acknowledging that He is in control.

Time with the One You Love

When a couple gets married, their greatest desire is to spend time together. Like a plant without water, a relationship without quality and quantity time together can wither and die. When husbands and wives put their relationship first, they feel appreciated, important and loved. Spending time with your spouse says, "You matter to me." Time together gives couples opportunities to renew their love, share their hopes and dreams, as well as their fears and failings.

This communication involves both speaking and listening. This past summer, LaVerne and I took a week to go to Florida just to be together, talk to each other, listen to each other and relax. Due to my intense travel schedule, we cherish these times away.

One night, over an evening meal at a beautiful spot near the ocean, LaVerne decided that she was going to see how long I would go without talking. She is definitely the conversation initiator in our relationship. We had a wonderful meal together (at least from my perspective); however, after the meal was over, she informed me that I had not shared a single word during the entire meal. I couldn't believe it! I guess I was focusing on other things without realizing how it took away from our time together.

The next dinner, I made up for it and talked nonstop. I overdid it, and she was ready for me to shut up. When I told my son-in-law this story, he said the greatest miracle was that his mother-in-law could go for a whole meal without talking!

Our God wants to spend time with us. He loves us dearly and completely. He wants us to have communion with Him. This is a two-way relationship. Sometimes we may express that relationship by being quiet and listening. Other times we may talk or weep or sing. We've been created to praise and commune with our wonderful heavenly Daddy, and no two days in our relationship will be alike!

Living a life of praise and thanksgiving opens our hearts to hear the voice of God. The disciples on the road to Emmaus invited Jesus into their home, but only after they gave thanks did they recognize it was really Him! As we give praise to our God in all situations, we will recognize the voice of God.

Apply What You've Learned

VERSE TO REMEMBER:

Through Jesus, therefore, let us continually offer to God a sacrifice of praise— the fruit of lips that confess his name.
HEBREWS 13:15

1. Tell of a time when you didn't feel like offering praise to God but did it anyway. What happened?

2. Did praising God ever help you defeat criticism, depression or fear so that you could hear God's voice more clearly? Give an example.

3. How does living a life of praise release the presence of God in your life?

5

Surrender

Like most of us, my friend Josh depended on his driver's license on a daily basis. So when he received a notice stating that he would lose his license for a year due to a prior citation, Josh was understandably eager to appeal his case. The night before the hearing, he earnestly prayed, and as an act of surrender said, "Lord, I give up my rights to my driver's license. I know I made a mistake, and I trust You."

When Josh arrived at the courthouse, the officer approached him and out of the blue announced that he was going to drop the charge. They proceeded to the judge to make everything official, and when the judge asked the officer why he was dropping the charge, he said, "I just want to help the guy out." The judge dismissed the case! Josh was overwhelmed with God's goodness to him. He knew somehow that his complete surrender allowed the Lord to work through him in a unique and awesome way.

Jesus surrendered His life; He gave it up freely and willingly so that you and I could have eternal life. It was the ultimate act of surrender. He didn't just give in or give up. The gospel of John reveals that Jesus said, "It is finished." Then *"he bowed his head* and gave up his spirit" (John 19:30, emphasis added).

Jesus bowed His head as an act of surrender.

Surrender opens the door for God to change us at the deepest level of our being and hear what He is saying to us. Surrender means to yield ownership, to relinquish control over what we consider ours: our property, our time and our rights. Without total surrender, we attempt to work for God instead of letting God work through us. When we surrender to God, we are simply acknowledging that our very life belongs to Him.

Let God Call the Shots!

We are generally self-centered rather than God-centered. But when we surrender our life to Jesus, our desires become more aligned with His. We learn to surrender as we walk hand in hand with Jesus. Of course, we do this by the Holy Spirit's power! John said, "By myself I can do nothing" (John 5:30). Paul agreed with John. He said he had to put his carnal nature to death every single day: "I die every day" (1 Cor. 15:31).

Allowing God to run your life with every breath you take means that you are trusting God the Father to fully handle your life. God wants to call the shots. He knows best, because He is God.

Joshua is a first-rate example of someone who fully surrendered to God. He is well known for having said, "As for me and my household, we will serve the LORD" (Josh. 24:15). Joshua knew that he had to make a choice about how to live his life: either by serving himself and his own wants and desires, or by fully serving God the Father. Joshua announced that he and his household's choice was surrender to God.

As well, Joshua encouraged those he led to make the same choice; he told them they must serve God with all their heart if they served Him at all. "Choose for yourselves this day whom you will serve" (Josh. 24:15). At the end of his life, Joshua said that God had not failed to give him every ounce of land that his foot had stepped on. God was able to do this because Joshua had fully surrendered and followed God every step of the way.

The Impossible Is Possible with God

This brings us to an important question. Is total surrender possible? Is it possible to put to death all of our desires and surrender fully? It's scary to give up personal control and hand it to God. Even if we are doing a lousy job of trying to run our own life, we'd rather stay in control. One reason is because surrendering to God requires obedience; and we don't always want to obey.

When a religious leader came to Jesus to ask what he must do to get to heaven, Jesus told him to sell all that he had and follow Him. The leader was not willing to surrender so completely and give up all he owned to follow Jesus, because he was very rich. Jesus turned to His disciples and said that it is hard for the rich to enter the kingdom of God. The disciples were astonished and wondered how anyone could be saved if it's that difficult! Jesus gave this answer: "What is impossible with men is possible with God" (Luke 18:27).

It's clear from this story that turning our lives over to God in total surrender is impossible for us to do. But Jesus said that "what is impossible with men is possible with God!" So we have hope. We have more than hope; we have a promise! If we surrender and then obey, we soon realize that Jesus can run our lives much better than we can!

Surrender and Wait

Surrender often involves time spent with God, waiting. "Those who wait on the Lord shall renew their strength" (Isa. 40:31, *NKJV*). Waiting on the Lord is surrendering to God.

The Bible says, "Trust in the Lord with all your heart and lean not on your own understanding; in all your ways acknowledge him, and he will make your paths straight" (Prov. 3:5-6). The word "all" means *all*. If we want divine guidance in our life, we must acknowledge Him as the Lord over all areas of life.

No matter what your circumstances, if you really surrender them to the Lord, you can rest in the knowledge that God is in charge and knows what you need. He will see you through so that His will be done.

Jesus said, "Come to me, all you who are weary and burdened, and I will give you rest. . . . For my yoke is easy and my burden is light" (Matt. 11:28-30). Jesus invites us to rest in quiet submission to Him and His will. When we rest, God will reveal those things that stand in our way of surrendering to Him.

Surrender and Rest

Learning to rest requires heaping "all your anxiety on him because he cares for you" (1 Pet. 5:7). When our house was first built, there were stones that needed to be removed before we could have a flourishing lawn. Because my dad owned the field next to our home, he said he wouldn't mind if we threw the rocks from our property into his adjacent field. So we did. That's a picture of what our heavenly Father wants us to do—throw our cares onto Him (He doesn't mind!), because He cares for us. Surrender and rest go hand in hand.

Surrender and Be Content

Submission also includes learning to be content with our current circumstances (see Phil. 4:11). When I travel to developing nations, there are times when I sleep in very poor conditions (one time I slept in a corn crib!), and at other times I am blessed to stay at a beautiful hotel. Either way, God has taught me to be content with every circumstance. This Scripture does not say we need to delight in the circumstances but that we should be able to say, "Lord, I know that You are in charge. I am satisfied with Your provision and goodness and what You determine is best for me now. Therefore, I am perfectly content."

It's when we turn away from what God intends for our lives and grumble and complain that we lose our peace and contentment. When we surrender in quiet trust, we find the benefits of God's grace and rest, and put ourselves in a position to hear His voice.

Sweet Surrender

One of the chief obstacles to surrendering is our fear of losing control. Recently, a squad of police in our county entered a home to confiscate a computer that was being used for illegal activity. One of the men living in the home, in a state of fear and in an attempt to protect his accused brother, locked himself in his bedroom with the computer and refused to give it up. The police broke down the door and, after a scuffle, he was arrested and taken into custody. All he had to do was give up the computer, but he could not clearly hear the officers' voices or understand their motives, and fear kept him from surrendering.

Fear, which keeps us in a state of confusion or anxiety, prevents us from surrendering to the Lord. We must remember God's words to us: "There is no fear in love. But perfect love drives out fear" (1 John 4:18). He loves us! God wants to speak to us if we will place ourselves in a position of continual surrender to Him. Listen to His voice in the midst of the noise and hear what He is saying. The act of surrendering allows the hand of God to influence our thoughts and feelings so that we can walk free in sweet surrender to Jesus.

Apply What You've Learned

VERSE TO REMEMBER:

In everything you do, put God first, and he will direct you.
PROVERBS 3:5-6, *TLB*

1. Since the day you gave your life to Jesus, how have your desires become more like His desires?

2. How does putting God first allow Him to direct you (speak to you)?

3. Describe a time when you surrendered to the Lord, waiting in trust until you could hear His voice.

6

Confession

In today's voyeuristic reality show environment, there are those who seem eager to confess their shortcomings for the entire world to see and hear. The more blatant the sin, the more response it gets from the audience. Then there are online sites that invite people to share their secrets and confessions anonymously.

But what is true confession? The New Testament Greek word for "confess" means *to agree with God* concerning His opinion of a matter. It also means *to admit guilt.* Confession acknowledges that we really do need God's forgiveness. When we confess our sins, we are agreeing with God concerning the sin in our life, as revealed through His Word by the Holy Spirit. Confession requires verbalizing our spiritual short-comings and admitting that we have sinned.

At no other time during prayer does the believer look so carefully at his own spiritual growth as during confession. Both King David and King Solomon spoke of this as communing with the heart.

The basic requirement for confession is to have the intention of returning to God. Confession alone is not enough. Confessing your sin means acknowledging your sin with true sorrow and intending for God to change you.

Sin builds a wall between you and God. If any sin remains uncon-fessed, you will be weighed down by it and eventually the sin will para-lyze you. To make matters worse, the Scriptures teach that if we have sin in our life, the Lord may not be listening to our prayers. King David said:

> If I had cherished sin in my heart, the Lord would not have listened; but God has surely listened and heard my voice in prayer. Praise be to God, who has not rejected my prayer or withheld his love from me! (Ps. 66:18-20).

How do we move from sin to forgiveness—that is, how do we access the amazing forgiveness of God? It is simple—we ask for it! In the church, we usually call this aspect of prayer "confession."

Healing for Your Heart

If we are going to hear the Lord speak to us, we must daily endeavor to keep our hearts pure. Someone once said that every major spiritual failure begins as a tiny seed of misconduct. During your times of confession, be on guard for little things—those tiny seeds of misconduct and attitudes that can grow to cause severe damage. A hidden or unnoticed sin has the potential to cause disorder and destruction in our life.

To make sure that we're sweeping away anything that could cause disorder, we should do a spiritual housecleaning every day. This kind of housekeeping goes beyond what others see and hear. It's not just a light dusting; it is a cleansing from within that takes place when we ask the Lord to cleanse those sins that we are not even aware of so that they can be rooted out and confessed and forgiven. This keeps our hearts spiritually healthy.

Confession is a condition of cleansing. The Bible encourages us to confess our sin and reach out for help. When our spiritual closets are clean, the heaviness from hidden sin lifts, and we are healed. We don't have to wait until our sin has completely weighed us down. We can come daily before the Lord and lay our sins at the foot of the Cross. Because we are far from perfect, confession is an ongoing activity. When we confess our sins, God wants us to be real with ourselves and with Him. The Bible says:

> If we claim to be without sin, we deceive ourselves and the truth is not in us. If we confess our sins, he is faithful and just and will forgive us our sins and purify us from all unrighteousness. If we claim we have not sinned, we make him out to be a liar and His Word has no place in our lives. My dear children, I write this to you so that you will not sin. But if anybody does sin, we have one who speaks to the Father in our defense—Jesus Christ, the Righteous One. He is the atoning sacrifice for our sins, and not only for ours but also for the sins of the whole world (1 John 1:8-10; 2:1-2).

The Devil Condemns, but God Convicts

Sometimes people struggle with false guilt, which feels like guilt but is really just shame. False guilt is the leftover negative feelings from our sinful past. False guilt causes us to hang on to feelings of being dirty and sinful, even after we have confessed our sin and God has forgiven us.

Before I received Jesus as my Lord, I experienced genuine guilt over my sins. Yet even after I received the Lord, the guilt continued, although from God's perspective, I was totally forgiven. Then I read God's Word: "If we confess our sins, he is faithful and just and will forgive us our sins and purify us from all unrighteousness" (1 John 1:9). I realized that I was plagued with false guilt, so I took the promise of 1 John 1:9 literally and confessed this Scripture aloud, over and over again, until faith rose up in my spirit and I really believed it.

I finally stopped living by past experiences, feelings and fears. I started living by the Word of God, and the guilt left. I knew that I was forgiven because the Bible told me I was! I remembered that God had "removed my sins as far as the east is from the west" (Ps. 103:12). I was safe from all condemnation for my sins. It was as if they had not been committed at all. That is how freely God forgives us when we place our trust in Him!

In contrast, the devil will tell us that it is a long way back to God when we sin. He will try to make us believe that God will never use us again. But we now know better. If we sin, we must confess our sin and repent (we stop and change our direction). The Lord forgives us, and we start again with a clean slate.

When our oldest daughter, Katrina, was about three years old, she could not hear properly in her right ear, so we took her to the family doctor. After giving her a thorough examination, he took a tube of water and shot it into her ear. Would you believe that a wad of paper came out?! It had been lodged deeply within her ear canal and could not be seen by simply peering into her ear. We had no idea the wad of paper was there, impairing her ability to hear.

Sin can keep us from hearing God's voice clearly. Our pipeline to heaven gets clogged. Sometimes, only the Great Physician can see the obstruction and take it out so that we can hear clearly once again.

David's prayers are good ones for all of us to pray: "See if there is any wicked way in me, and lead me in the way everlasting" (Ps. 139:24, *NKJV*); "Create in me a pure heart, O God, and renew a steadfast spirit within me" (Ps. 51:10).

Apply What You've Learned

VERSE TO REMEMBER:

He would not have listened if I had not confessed my sins. But he listened!
He heard my prayer! He paid attention to it!
PSALM 66:18-20, *TLB*

1. How does unconfessed sin keep you from hearing from God?

2. Describe a time when your "pipeline" to God became unclogged as a result of confessing sin in your life.

3. Pray the prayer in Psalms 139:24 and 51:10.

7

Worship

You were made for fellowship with God, and your heart will never be satisfied without it. God wants you to love Him deeply and bring pleasure to Him through your worship and devotion. The Bible says, "The Lord is pleased only with those who worship him and trust his love" (Ps. 147:11, *CEV*).

Jesus responds to your worship. One day a sinful woman came to Jesus, weeping. Her heart was deeply stirred with her love for Jesus, and she stood crying beside him with her tears wetting his feet. She then knelt down and kissed his feet as she poured an expensive perfume on them, revealing her lavish love for her Lord. This woman had tried to fulfill her longing for love from men, but now she had found the Lover of her soul. She was not ashamed to express that love openly and freely. She knew that she could trust the Lord.

Indeed, upon receiving her act of worship, Jesus spoke to her. He responded to her worship by telling her that her sins were forgiven and that she should go in peace (see Luke 7:36-50).

Worship is a lifelong conversation and love affair between you and God as you surrender your life to Him. Worship is often mistakenly relegated only to our participation in a church service when we praise and worship the Lord. Of course, when we surrender our hearts to the Lord and worship Him with music and singing in a church service, we will hear God's voice, but worship involves so much more.

God Speaks in Your Worship

Worship is a lifestyle of bringing pleasure to God through the way you live. Rick Warren wrote, "Every activity can be transformed into an act of worship when you do it for the praise, glory, and pleasure of God."[1] The Bible says, "So whether you eat or drink or whatever you do, do it all for the glory of God" (1 Cor. 10:31).

Martin Luther observed, "A dairymaid can milk cows to the glory of God." Olympic runner Eric Liddel maintained, "When I run, I feel his pleasure." For Liddell, running was an act of worship.

Because worship is a function of the heart, there really are no formulas for worship. If you do everything as if you are doing it for Jesus, then even everyday chores are an act of worship.

Jesus said that all worship must take place "in spirit and in truth" (John 4:24). We communicate with God through our spirit. Our spirit intuitively senses God's presence and receives revelation from Him.

Sometimes the lyrics of a song suddenly become personal to your life, giving insight or direction in a timely way. You may be listening to a worship music CD, participating in a worship service or mowing your lawn when the Lord speaks clearly to you. Because you are focusing on Him and giving Him your undivided attention and love, you are in a position to hear clearly what the Lord is speaking to you.

"God often speaks to me through songs," says Joann, who serves in our family of churches. "There are times when I don't know how to pray for situations that are happening to me, and God brings a specific song to my remembrance. As I sing out the lyrics, I realize the words have direct impact for the situation I am in."

When you live a life of worship to your God, He is in the midst of it. But the devil, who dwells in darkness, hates it when we worship God, because it reminds him of his past when he was overseeing the choirs of heaven. Amy Carmichael said, "I believe truly that Satan cannot endure it and so slips out of the room—more or less!—when there is a true song. Prayer rises more easily, more spontaneously, after one has let those wings, words, and music, carry one out of oneself into that upper air."[2]

When we are "carried into that upper air," joyfully basking in the presence of God, we will hear God speak. I often receive messages from the Lord while I am worshiping in His presence. When the Lord called me to start a new church in my twenties, it was during a worship service in my local church in Pennsylvania.

If you are worshiping the Lord, and He speaks something to you, write down what He says. His words might be for today, next month, a year from now or a decade from now. Write it down so that you won't forget what the Lord has spoken. Later, and often many years later, you will be wonderfully surprised at what He told you.

The Role of Thankfulness

Thankfulness is an act of worship. God's general will for you is to "give thanks in all circumstances; for this is the will of God in Christ Jesus for you" (1 Thess. 5:18, *RSV*). When you have learned to obey His will today by being thankful, you don't have to worry about what God will speak to you tomorrow. You will be ready today to hear His voice in the future. Thankfulness keeps our ears and mind open to God's voice. The Bible says that we are to thank God *in* everything, not *for* everything. That means that no matter what is going on, we are not to complain, murmur, grumble or find fault. God doesn't want to hear us grumbling, because grumbling is evidence that we have no faith in His ability to make things better.

After telling us to thank God in everything, the very next verse says, "Do not quench the Spirit" (1 Thess. 5:19, *RSV*). We can quench the Holy Spirit's voice in us through complaining. Grumblers have a very hard time hearing from God. The Bible says, "Do everything without complaining or arguing" (Phil. 2:14-15). It's our natural tendency to complain; we all do it at one time or another. But it is unnatural or even supernatural to give thanks amidst life's tests and trials.

Worship gets our eyes off of our problems and onto the Lord Jesus. It is self-correcting, like a clock that resets itself to the right time every 24 hours. We should choose to worship every day, because giving thanks is the will of God for all of us. Unthankful people quickly enter into deception and find it very hard to hear the clear, pure word of the Lord.

Jesus said, "If you remain in me and my words remain in you, ask whatever you wish, and it will be given you" (John 15:7). God wants our hearts. Jesus did not fail to respond to the woman who anointed His feet with perfume as her act of worship and adoration. When you worship Him, He will respond to you too. He is eager to speak to you. Just love Him!

Apply What You've Learned

VERSE TO REMEMBER:

The Lord is pleased only with those who worship him and trust his love.

PSALM 147:11, *CEV*

1. Describe how you can make worship a lifestyle.

2. How has God spoken to you through your times of worship?

3. Explain how thankfulness keeps our minds open to hearing from God.

Notes
1. Rick Warren, *The Purpose Driven Life* (Grand Rapids, MI: Zondervan, 2002), p. 67.
2. Donald E. Demaray, *Alive to God Through Prayer* (Grand Rapids, MI: Baker Book House, 1965), p. 27.

8

Asking in Prayer

There are no matters too small or insignificant to God. He cares about the major and minor things in our lives; He is concerned about the smallest detail. So pray about everything! I believe that God loves to respond even to a simple prayer like, "Please help me find my car keys, Lord." Scripture advises us to pray before we do anything else. "I urge, then, first of all, that requests, prayers, intercession and thanksgiving be made for everyone" (1 Tim. 2:1).

My friend Allen, a pastor, says that this lesson of immediately praying for everything was amplified for him during a mission trip to Kenya. The van they were driving refused to start. Not having the tools or the skills to work on the van, Allen felt quite helpless watching others work on it. Then he heard the Lord say, "Have you prayed?" Immediately, Allen suggested they lay hands on the van and pray. After a simple prayer asking God to fix the van, they tried the engine, and it started! Amazed smiles lit the faces around them as they realized what had just happened.

Pray for large and small things. Pray for healing for a cough or cold before getting out the medicine. Pray for cars and dishwashers and computers. Pray for the people around you. Pray, pray, pray!

God Speaks in Response to Prayer

Regardless of the different ways that God communicates with us, He often speaks to us in response to prayer. Psalm 91:15 tells us that when we call on Him, He will answer. Cornell Haan, cofounder of the World Prayer Team, recalls how his mother would sit in her chair praying when, as a rebellious teenager, he arrived home after curfew.

> She did not scold me, but simply sat with tears in her eyes, praying for me. It caused me to be very ashamed of my disobedience—more so than a sharp talking to or being grounded. From her I learned to pray about problems more and to speak harshly less.[1]

God heard and answered this mother's prayers, and her son's life was changed. Our prayers keep us on God's mind. He notices our heartfelt requests.

In the book of Acts, we read that God spoke to Cornelius in response to his sincere prayers. "Four days ago I was in my house praying. . . . Suddenly a man in shining clothes stood before me and said, 'Cornelius, God has heard your prayer and remembered your gifts to the poor. Send to Joppa for Simon who is called Peter'" (Acts 10:30-32).

Cornelius, a Gentile, was not yet a believer in Jesus Christ when he prayed and God noticed and spoke to him. God sent an angel to tell Cornelius to invite a Jewish stranger to his home who would tell him about Jesus. God loves to answer us when we pray sincere prayers to Him.

The parents of John the Baptist heard God speak in answer to their prayers. "Then an angel of the Lord appeared to him, standing at the right side of the altar of incense. When Zechariah saw him, he was startled and was gripped with fear. But the angel said to him: 'Do not be afraid, Zechariah; your prayer has been heard. Your wife Elizabeth will bear you a son, and you are to give him the name John'" (Luke 1:11-13).

Pray with Perseverence!

Jesus told two stories in the book of Luke that emphasize the importance of continuing a determined perseverance in prayer. In the first story he said:

> Suppose one of you has a friend, and he goes to him at midnight and says, "Friend, lend me three loaves of bread, because a friend of mine on a journey has come to me, and I have nothing to set before him." Then the one inside answers, "Don't bother me. The door is already locked, and my children are with me in bed. I can't get up and give you anything." I tell you, though he will not get up and give him the bread because he is his friend, yet because of the man's boldness he will get up and give him as much as he needs (Luke 11:5-8).

Just as this man gave in after repeated requests from his friend, so our God will respond after our persistent prayer. Jesus went on to say, "Ask and it will be given to you; seek and you will find; knock and the door will be opened to you. For everyone who asks receives; he who seeks finds; and to him who knocks, the door will be opened" (Luke 11:9-10).

We must ask in order to receive an answer. When we seek Him, we will find Him. When we continue to knock, God will answer. The Bible tells us that we do not have because we do not ask (see Jas. 4:2-3).

The second story Jesus told His disciples about persevering included a judge who "neither feared God nor cared about men."

And there was a widow in that town who kept coming to him with the plea, "Grant me justice against my adversary." For some time he refused. But finally he said to himself, "Even though I don't fear God or care about men, yet because this widow keeps bothering me, I will see that she gets justice, so that she won't eventually wear me out with her coming!" And the Lord said . . . "And will not God bring about justice for his chosen ones, who cry out to him day and night?" (Luke 18:3-7).

If we feel that we seldom hear from God, perhaps we have stopped asking. God loves to answer our prayers, but sometimes there is a waiting time between our asking and receiving the answer. Nonetheless, we need to persevere. Melody and her husband, who lived in Indiana, prayed for seven years to have children. They finally were led to adopt a baby girl from Russia. Shortly thereafter, Melody got pregnant and had another daughter. A few years later she again gave birth to a third daughter! In describing how God had answered their prayers, Melody found herself telling a friend, "After all these years of praying, God finally answered our prayers." But the Holy Spirit immediately spoke to her spirit, saying, "No, I answered you the first time you asked, and my answer was yes, but it is just now coming to pass." God had answered their prayers, but there was a waiting time between their asking and receiving the answer. That's where perseverance pays off. If we do not lose hope, God will speak, one way or another, and we will hear Him!

Bring Your Shopping List

Sometimes when we ask the Lord for the things we need, we may feel like we are bringing a "shopping list" to him. But God wants us to ask. He tells us that we do not have because we do not ask Him (see Jas. 4:2). He desires to provide for us, and He wants us to ask daily. We can be confident that God will provide. In the wilderness, God provided daily sustenance for the Israelites in the form of manna. God is no less concerned for us. Just as He daily provided manna for Israel, He promises us our daily bread (see Matt. 6:11). We must trust in His provision, and not our own.

Speaking of daily provision, it is interesting to note that the Israelites could not store up the manna for a rainy day; they could only take one day's worth of manna at a time, because yesterday's manna would be stale if they tried to store it. The same is true of our relationship with the Lord. We position ourselves to receive from Him daily. Yesterday's experience with God was yesterday's experience. Today we have to draw close to God again for the day's nourishment. He sustains us just one day at a time. That's what keeps our relationship with Him fresh and growing.

In Matthew 6:25-34, Jesus exhorted His followers not to be preoccupied with food and clothing; instead He invited them to depend on God, like the birds and the wildflowers depend on Him. Since God provides sustenance for birds that do not have the ability to sow, reap and store, how much more can we, who have been provided with these abilities, trust our heavenly Father to take care of us!

In other words, we do not have to be anxious in our asking. Rather, God instructs us to have a constant attitude of thanksgiving. Philippians 4:6 tells us that we should "not be anxious about anything, but in everything, by prayer and petition, with thanksgiving, present [our] requests to God."

God is faithful, even in the small things we encounter in the day-to-day grind of life. A young man that I know had a deadline to finish a job for a customer when he discovered the fuel in his air compressor was very low. It was almost a certainty that he would run out of gas and his work day would be greatly prolonged. So he prayed that God would allow the gas to last until the job was completed. Two full hours later, he finished the job, and the gas finally ran out. I believe that God loves for us to ask in prayer, because He is a faithful prayer-answering God!

Apply What You've Learned

VERSE TO REMEMBER:

Call upon me, and I will answer.
PSALM 91:15

1. Give an example of how God has spoken to you in response to prayer.
2. Why is it important to persevere in prayer?
3. What should be our attitude when we ask in prayer?

Note
1. Cornell Haan, "Which Intercessor Most Influenced Your Prayer Life?" *Charisma*, September/October 2004, p. 14.

Section Three

SPIRITUAL PERCEPTION

9

His Peace

As a child, Naomi enjoyed sitting on the couch behind the space heater on a cold winter's evening. The warmth often lulled her to sleep. When she awoke in the morning, she would be in her own bed, and most of the time, she didn't remember how she got there. Occasionally, she would awaken to feel her papa tenderly lifting her in his big arms and settling her in her bed for the night. Her feeling of peace and well-being soon had her sound asleep again.

Have you learned to let God do for you what Naomi's papa did for her? God wants to "carry you" and have you rest in His care and provision. Too often, we work too hard to figure things out. But God wants us to rest, to be at peace, and trust Him while He does His work in our life.

Jesus spoke of the kind of peace He offers when He said, "Peace I leave with you; my peace I give you. I do not give to you as the world gives. Do not let your hearts be troubled and do not be afraid" (John 14:27).

When we really believe and trust, having confidence in God, we will not feel worry or fear in our heart. Peace is the result of trusting completely. The Bible says that God's peace surpasses human comprehension (see Phil. 4:7). As we learn to hear the voice of God, a distinct calmness will fill our heart.

Inner peace comes from an unwavering trust in Jesus. When our trust is in Him who is our only true source of peace, He dispels the fears that can grip us in an uncertain world and often result from our own faults and failures. It is only through faith in Jesus and in the work that He did on the cross that we can know the supernatural peace He promises to give us.

The Bible says, "Let the peace of Christ rule in your hearts, since as members of one body you were called to peace. And be thankful" (Col. 3:15). The word "rule" literally means "to be an umpire." In other words, the peace of God in our hearts is an umpire that guides us to make decisions.

A lack of peace may be the Holy Spirit warning us that we should not move forward in a particular direction. The peace of God in our heart is often described as a "gut" feeling that will lead us to make the right decisions.

A man was offered a job by a large company, the salary of which was considerably more money than he had ever made in his life. As he considered the offer, he thought of all the wonderful philanthropic things he could do with the extra money: use it to help friends, give to the poor, help the homeless. In his gut, however, he did not have peace from God about taking the job, so he turned it down.

The president of the company thought he was crazy, as did some of his friends. It seemed like a once-in-a-lifetime opportunity; but he could not take the job without the blessing of God. A short time later, it was discovered that the president of the company had committed many illegal dealings, and the whole company was in trouble. If the man had taken the job, he might have been implicated just because he worked there. At the very least, he would have had to choose between being honest and keeping the job. God kept this man from getting involved in a very unpleasant situation.

Several years ago, a friend told me that he wanted to give me his car as a gift. It was a beautiful car; but my wife, LaVerne, and I did not have the peace of God in our hearts to receive it, so we graciously declined his offer. Some time later, the Lord provided our family with a customized van, and this time we had the peace to receive it from the benefactor. Had we received the car, we would not have been offered the van, which was the perfect vehicle at the time for our growing family.

Almost every weekend I speak at a different church, in a different city, somewhere in the world. How do I know which invitations to accept and which ones to decline? I often depend on the peace of God. When I am asked to speak and do not have the peace of God in my spirit, I decline. I have learned over the years that it always pays to obey the peace that God places in my heart.

Recently, I had the privilege of investing some money into a business that paid great dividends. I was ready to reinvest the money into the same company again; but LaVerne did not have peace about it. I have learned to listen to what the Lord speaks to my wife, so I did not reinvest. We later discovered that the company was involved in massive financial difficulties, and had I invested money into it, I would have lost every cent I put in. We followed our lack of peace and the Lord used it to protect us.

I was talking to a friend who is struggling with God's will regarding which church to attend in his community. I simply encouraged him to follow the peace of God in his heart, because the Bible says, "And the peace of God, which transcends all understanding, will guard your hearts and your minds in Christ Jesus" (Phil. 4:7).

Remember, when the deceiver speaks to us, he cannot give true peace. When we try to make decisions only with our own reasoning, we cannot get true peace. You don't have to explain to other people why you don't have peace about a certain thing; sometimes you won't even know why yourself.

Even when you believe that God has spoken, you should wait until peace fills your heart to do what you believe He has instructed you. In this way, you are assured that your timing is right. Peace is a confirmation that you are hearing from the Lord. If I am shopping with my wife, we don't buy something if we don't have peace about it. If we are working on a particular project and start to feel uneasy about it, we are not acting from faith if we continue to push on without examining why peace has dissipated.

Peace is closely tied to "conviction," which we will examine in chapter 11. I like the way this teacher of the Word shows the connection:

> It doesn't work to use the excuse that everyone else does what we're convicted not to do. Many of God's people are powerless because they continually do things their conscience tells them not to do. When we don't pay heed to our conscience, we lose our peace (see Romans 14:23).[1]

We should never act without peace; it is a vital ingredient to hearing God's voice. Peace is an internal confirmation that the action being taken is approved of by God. Obeying the peace of God in our heart allows us to carry on with a sense of His acceptance and favor.

Apply What You've Learned

VERSE TO REMEMBER:

Let the peace of Christ rule in your hearts, since as members of one body you were called to peace.
COLOSSIANS 3:15

1. Think of a time when your heart was unsettled and you did not make a decision because you didn't have a peace about it. Was it God speaking?

2. Can you describe the inner peace that comes from trusting Jesus?

3. How do "peace" and "conviction" go hand in hand when it comes to hearing from God?

Note

1. Joyce Meyer, *How to Hear from God* (New York: Time Warner Book Group, 2003), p. 85.

10

His Still, Small Voice

Brenda was spring-cleaning her basement when she heard God's still, small voice: "Go pray for Georgia." The voice was so clear that Brenda looked around to see if someone was standing there. Realizing that it was God speaking, Brenda put down her cleaning supplies and walked over to her neighbor Georgia's house. She didn't know Georgia well, but she knew that Georgia had cancer and was quite ill. "The Lord told me to come over and pray for you, Georgia. May I?" Brenda asked.

"I would like that!" Georgia said, and invited her in. Brenda prayed a simple, short prayer, asking the Lord that the next appointment Georgia had with the doctor would show the cancer gone. It happened as God had spoken; the cancer was completely gone at her next appointment. Brenda was thrilled to know that she had listened to God's still, small voice, and He had heard her! God is at work on this earth, and He wants to involve us in what He is doing.

When we use the catchphrase that God speaks through a "still, small voice," it comes from the story of Elijah (see 1 Kings 19:11-13, *AMP*), when God spoke to him in the quiet of his heart. Elijah discovered that when God was not heard in the mighty wind, earthquake or fire, he heard him speak with the sound of a gentle whisper known to his heart.

The quiet whisper captured Elijah's attention because it was a tender communication from a loving Father who came to encourage him in a personal way. This steady inner voice gave him specific guidance in a time of need.

Many times, we are looking for the Lord to speak to us in an earth-shattering way; but He usually speaks to us by His Spirit, deep within our own spirit, through Holy Spirit-inspired impressions, thoughts and feelings. It is imperative that we pay attention to those impressions that come to us clearly. For example, have you ever found yourself experiencing a spontaneous thought that you should pray for someone? Most likely, God was speaking to you in His still, small voice. God often speaks quietly to our spirits, nudging us to obedience to His voice.

Many of the major decisions in my life have come as a result of that quiet voice. When I was in my twenties, and the Lord began to speak to me about starting a church with small groups, He asked, "Are you willing to be involved in the underground church?" It was not a booming voice in an earthquake; it was a "still, small voice." The "voice" was very clear—and it changed the direction of my life.

The Inner Witness of the Holy Spirit

If there is a "usual" way that God speaks to us, it's probably through that inner voice of the Holy Spirit. Some people are quite attuned to this still, small voice and hear it regularly. Others only hear it once in a while. It's easy to get so caught up in all the activities of life that we just don't take time to listen. If we take the time to slow down and acknowledge the Lord, He will have something to say to us. Sometimes it may be simply the assurance of, "You're doing fine. Just keep going."

Sensitivity to the Holy Spirit causes us to hear when He speaks. A friend of mine who is a new believer recently destroyed his drug paraphernalia because God spoke to him through His still, small voice, gently nudging him to break this stronghold in his life.

There are times when I am picking up something for my family at the grocery store and a still, small voice tells me to purchase an extra item not on the list. Nearly always, when I get home, the item that I chose was needed. On one occasion, the Holy Spirit asked me to give some money to a missionary family. I was later informed that they had no money for food. Obviously, this gift was a direct answer to their desperate prayers.

The Lord desires to speak to us by this witness of His Spirit. The Bible says, "The Spirit himself testifies with our spirit that we are God's children" (Rom. 8:16). The mind receives head knowledge, but the spirit receives a deeper sense of knowing by the Holy Spirit. I believe there are things we know through head knowledge, but there are also things we know because the Holy Spirit communicates them to us. For example, many times when I am teaching, the Lord drops a new thought into my spirit that I share, but it was not in my notes.

This is God speaking through the Holy Spirit in His still, small voice that causes me to be sensitive to Him.

A few years ago, our daughter Leticia, along with four friends, was involved in an auto accident in which their car was broadsided by an 18-wheeler traveling at 55 miles per hour. One girl's grandmother awakened at 11:20 P.M. and felt she should pray for the safety of her granddaughter. It turned out that this inner witness of the Holy Spirit nudged her to pray during the exact time of the accident. I truly believe that because she listened to God's still, small voice and prayed, no one was seriously hurt in this potentially deadly accident.

God's Impulses

Many times we hear a voice within us but excuse it as our own thought. It may be God! Take that inner voice seriously.

These divine or heavenly "nudges" are one way that God sends His messages to us. God gives these impulses to guide and encourage us in our walk with Him. They may be what some pass off as just coincidental, but after a while, God will confirm that these inner nudges of conviction are from Him.

The Bible says, "The lamp of the Lord searches the spirit of a man; it searches out his inmost being" (Prov. 20:27). Your spirit is a light that the Lord has illuminated. He will throw its rays into the darkest recesses of the heart so that you will know how to distinguish right from wrong. You can trust this "Holy Ghost flashlight" to hear God's still, small voice speak to you.

One of my friends tells me that he hears the Lord speak to him more often while mowing the lawn or taking a shower than at any other time. Why? We often hear God when we are doing some activity that has become automatic for us (exercising, cooking, cleaning) because our minds are free to receive through our spirits from the voice of the Holy Spirit.

An Intuitive Conviction

We often think that hearing God's voice is complicated, but it is really not as hard as one might think. Years ago, when my wife and I were preparing to become missionaries, we had two choices. Our mission board told us there were openings in the states of Connecticut and South Carolina. As we prayed, the Lord placed a burden on our hearts for the people on an island off the coast of South Carolina.

We didn't hear God speak in an audible voice, but the feeling seemed to be nudging us in a specific direction. We knew that it was the right place. We just had this sense in our spirits that it was right. God confirmed this intuitive conviction, and we served on John's Island, South Carolina, throughout the following year.

When we are really serious about listening to God, we can expect an answer from Him. The Scriptures tell us, "In his heart a man plans his course, but the Lord determines his steps" (Prov. 16:9). Look back at your life and see how the Lord has directed your steps. Sometimes God speaks to us by putting a desire or burden in our heart that we know would not come from anyone else but God. We just have a certain intuitive conviction about it that gives us faith.

Let God Capture Your Attention

Sheep follow their shepherd because they trust their shepherd's voice. They quickly become accustomed to their shepherd's particular inflections and sounds. Sheep can distinguish this voice from other voices, and although they will hear others, they will not follow the voice of a stranger. The sheep know that their shepherd cares for them and has their best interest in mind.

Scripture says that we follow our Shepherd because we "know his voice" (John 10:4). God speaks to those whose trust is completely in Him. Rest assured that you will learn to recognize this inner voice, this impression from the Lord, as you come to know His voice. Let Him capture your attention through a whisper. His voice is one of love and concern for your well-being. Listen for Him to speak in a still, small voice amidst the noise of everyday life.

Apply What You've Learned

VERSE TO REMEMBER:

The Lord passed by . . . a still small voice.
1 KINGS 19:11-12, *NKJV*

1. How does sensitivity to the inner witness of the Holy Spirit help you hear from God?

2. How have you learned to distinguish the sound of the Lord's whispers in your heart?

3. Has God ever prompted you to do something by an inner nudge that you recognized as His still, small voice in your spirit? Describe what happened.

11

Conviction

To all outward appearances, Jan was leading a charmed life. She was a responsible wife and mother, a competent employee and a church and choir member; but she was living a life that did not include God. Her whole life was a lie. She was addicted to alcohol and drugs, going from one high to the next and enduring an abusive marital relationship. Her life was empty, and she knew it.

One morning, she was alone in the house, walking down the hallway, when suddenly she was on the floor! She had not done any drugs. She had not fallen or fainted. Jan felt as if she were being held in place by a giant, invisible thumb! She could move, but she could not get up. Strangely enough, she was not afraid. A voice spoke to her, convicting her of her lifestyle. The voice said, "You have to make a choice—*My* way or *your* way. My way is life. If you choose my way, I'll set you free." Jan knew what the other choice was. She was living it. When she got up, she was changed forever. Any desire she had for alcohol or drugs was completely quenched. She had experienced the conviction of God!

God speaks to us by giving us an ever-deepening conviction and awareness of His presence in our daily life. He not only wants us to listen so that He can tell us what to do, but He also wants us to listen so that we know what not to do. This is His conviction.

Jesus said that He would send the Holy Spirit to indwell us and convict us of sin (see John 16:7-10). When the Holy Spirit convicts us, we see just how desperately we need God. He doesn't convict us of our sin to expose us and make us feel bad. Instead, He wants to make us feel desperate for Him, realizing that we have no confidence in ourselves.

Oswald Chambers wrote:

Conviction of sin is one of the most uncommon things that ever happens to a person. It is the beginning of an understanding of God.[1]

Conviction moves us to look at what God offers and challenges us to know this infinite, loving and almighty heavenly Father.

The Holy Spirit speaks to our conscience to convict us of any sin and gives us a disposition toward righteousness. His convicting work is intended to convince us to repent, which means to turn and go in the right direction.

In other words, if we are behaving in a way that is not pleasing to God, we must be willing to make an adjustment in our life. If we don't, our hearts become hardened. Hardened hearts are the result of ignoring the Holy Spirit's conviction of right and wrong. The more hard-hearted we become, the more difficult it is to quickly hear and promptly obey the Lord.

If I am angry at someone, bitterness can grow in my heart. If, however, I allow the Holy Spirit and the Word of God to quickly prompt me to forgive, I can receive grace to move on and hear the Lord speak to me. I can depend on God to convict me to do what is right.

A Transforming Adjustment

God loves to transform people. It is a promise in His Word. He said that He would remove our unnaturally hardened hearts and give us a heart of flesh, a heart that is sensitive to the touch of God (see Ezek. 36:26).

Some time after I received Jesus Christ as my Lord, the Holy Spirit convicted me of cheating when I remembered that I had deceived a classmate in high school. Another friend and I were gambling with him and had rigged it so that he always lost. I wrote to the classmate, explained what had happened and asked his forgiveness, returning the money that I had taken from him, with interest. God convicted me so that I could make an adjustment in my life and hear from Him with a clear conscience.

God is no respecter of persons when it comes to communicating with His children. Regardless of our age, each one of us is capable of hearing God's voice of conviction. One of our pastor's children, seven-year-old Bryce, was saving his money to buy a PlayStation 2 game for quite some time. Upon hearing a Bible lesson on "giving to God," he was convicted that he should give all of the money he had saved to God. He felt that he had heard God speak to him, so he obediently put all of his hard-earned money in the church offering. The next day, the very game Bryce had been saving for appeared on the windshield of the family's van with a note: "Bryce, you cannot outgive Me. I will always give you back more in return. Love, your heavenly Father." God spoke a valuable life lesson to Bryce about obeying that voice of conviction, which he will not soon forget.

Conviction vs. Condemnation

True conviction is entirely different from condemnation. God's voice of conviction over sin always gives us a way out. It's life-changing. The enemy's voice will bring condemnation with no way out, and no hope. For example, Satan may say to you, "You know, you never pray enough" or "If you would read your Bible more, God would love you more." Condemnation is shame-based and accuses us in our character.

Conviction from God arouses hope. It moves us beyond failure and causes us to want to know God more fully and deeply. It is about a specific sin, rather than a general accusation of character.

The devil condemns us, but God convicts us. Condemnation brings doubt, fear, unbelief and hopelessness. God convicts us in order to restore us to righteousness and faith. He always corrects us to build us up, and He provides a way of escape.

> No temptation has seized you except what is common to man. And God is faithful; he will not let you be tempted beyond what you can bear. But when you are tempted, he will also provide a way out so that you can stand up under it (1 Cor. 10:13).

It is so important to discern the truth and to know the difference between conviction and condemnation. If you respond to the Lord's conviction, you will be lifted up and out of sin; however, condemnation only makes you feel worse about yourself. It is healthy and normal to feel guilty when we are initially convicted of sin; however, if we keep feeling guilty after we have repented, it is spiritually unhealthy.

We could sum it up this way—conviction is God speaking to us about His limits, providing protection for us. Condemnation is Satan speaking to us to bring us into bondage to shame and false guilt.

The Finger of Conviction

It is good to know that the Holy Spirit doesn't spring everything on us at once. He usually convicts us to change or make adjustments in our life when He knows that we are ready, and His timing is incredible.

The Lord invites us to approach Him without fear. The Bible says that He wants to help us in our time of need. "Let us then approach the throne of grace with confidence, so that we may receive mercy and find grace to help us in our time of need" (Heb. 4:16). If there is sin in our life, our heavenly Father still loves us. He wants us to come boldly to His throne and receive His forgiveness, grace and mercy!

God's conviction fell on a bakery owner in Bristol, England, while George Müller was praying for food for his orphanages,[2] which relied solely on contributions to feed the children. The children were in dire need of food this day, and George was praying for this need. The Lord awakened a bakery owner across town who felt God's conviction to get up, call an employee and ask him to go to the shop to bake a day's amount of bread for the orphans. Then on second thought, he told the employee, "Bake enough for a month so that I can get some sleep."

God is speaking to us when He convicts us. This conviction might come from an inner prompting of His still, small voice; from reading the Word of God; from hearing a sermon preached; or in some other way. God convicts us so that we can be released to move forward in His grace and mercy as we continue to develop a sensitivity to hear His voice.

Apply What You've Learned

VERSE TO REMEMBER:

*When he comes, he will convict the world of guilt in regard to
sin and righteousness and judgment.*
JOHN 16:8

1. How does conviction stir your conscience to want to know God better?
2. Can you distinguish between condemnation and conviction of the Holy Spirit? If not, what can you do to make this distinction?
3. Describe a time when the Lord spoke to you through conviction.

Notes
1. Oswald Chambers, "My Utmost for His Highest Daily Devotional," RBC Ministries, 2007. http://www.rbc.org/utmost/index.php?month=12&day=07&year=07 (accessed October 2007).
2. George Müller (1805-1898) was an evangelist and coordinator of orphanages in Bristol, England. He cared for 10,024 orphans in his lifetime and was well known for his prayers of faith that worked miracles regarding the care of orphans.

12

Partial Revelation

A young man named Peter and a team of young people in Great Britain found themselves praying at a large art museum in the heart of London. Peter said, "It was one of those 'It is either God or I am crazy' moments. Whoever heard of walking through an art museum in prayer?" But they did it anyway, although it made no sense to them.

The following year, Peter returned to the same art museum to find a large banner with the words "Seeing Salvation." Intrigued, Peter walked into a number of rooms dedicated to paintings that showed different aspects of Jesus' life and ministry. There were Scripture verses in large letters around the walls; the gift shop was selling Bibles! Amazed, Peter remembered the teams' prayers. Although at the time they had only partially understood what God intended, now they knew. God had wanted to communicate Jesus to the people of London through an art exhibition—and they got to be part of it through prayer!

The Bible tells us that we all "know in part" (1 Cor. 13:9). It is not a weakness in our relationship with the Lord when we only have a piece of the puzzle. When the Lord speaks to us, everything is seldom crystal-clear. We often miss some of the details, and we sometimes make assumptions of what we believe the Lord has spoken.

Sometimes God speaks to our spirit, but our soul (mind, will and emotions) gets entangled with our inner voice. We get a message, but perhaps only a portion of it from the Lord. If you have ever taken a drink out of a garden hose, you will likely taste both the water and the rubber hose. This analogy applies to hearing from the Lord. Sometimes what we hear is partially the Lord and is, at the same time, partially us.

Incremental Guidance

Paul the apostle, as intimate as he was with God, did not always hear the entire message from the Lord all at one time. He had to take one step at a time. On one missionary journey, he and his companions were making their way toward Ephesus, but God stopped them. Then he started northward into Bithynia, and again God stopped him. Then he turned northwest and came to Troas. Finally, Paul had a dream and saw a man pleading with him to come to Macedonia, which was where God wanted him. Many people came to Christ there (see Acts 16). This is an example of incremental guidance by which Paul heard God's voice in part, and step by step he discovered the way God wanted him to go.

Abraham is another example of someone who trusted God to lead him one step at a time. His story beginning in Genesis 12:1 describes the start of his faith journey: "Now the Lord said to Abram, 'Go for yourself away from your country, from your relatives and your father's house, to the land that I will show you.'" God gave Abraham step one. God implied that Abraham wasn't getting step two or three until he had accomplished step one. This sounds like common sense, but it is so true: God usually gives us His direction one step at a time.

Many people run into a problem here. They refuse to take step one until they think they understand the next steps. But if we knew all the steps ahead of time, there would be no need for faith. Understanding this truth, that His will is usually revealed to us one step at a time, will build our confidence to do what we already know to do— which is to step out. After we take the first few steps, our faith will really begin to grow.

At times, we are stretched in faith as we step out to do things that we do not yet have experience doing or are not comfortable doing at first. No one is instantly a spiritual giant who can take great steps of faith. Faith grows and develops through experience.

Trust is so important when we take those faith steps. Did you ever ask God to supply a financial need and He came through, but only at the last minute? My experience is that many times the Lord gives us what we need at the very last moment because faith grows by waiting!

Obey Anyway

Faith is the bottom line when it comes to learning to hear the voice of the Lord. The Bible says, "Now faith is being sure of what we hope for and certain of what we do not see" (Heb. 11:1). A weatherman uses radar and satellite to predict a coming storm. He is sure the storm is coming, but he cannot prove it because it has not yet physically arrived. When the storm comes, it is no longer *faith*, but *reality*. Once we have a manifestation of what we desire in our circumstance, we no longer need faith in that area. But until we hear God's voice, we need faith!

Soldiers in military training are sometimes required to do things that simply do not make sense. Military boot camp is extremely difficult. It is designed to take the recruit to his or her limit. If, under extreme physical and mental pressure, the recruit does not fall apart, he or she may qualify for military service. If he or she does fall apart, the recruit will be sent home as "unfit for military service" and will never see or experience military life.

Why so harsh? New recruits must learn to obey quickly without questioning their superiors. If they are on the front lines of battle, and their leaders give them a command, they could seriously injure themselves or others if they turn to ask, "Why?" In the same way, God wants us to learn to trust Him and obey, even if it doesn't always make complete sense to us.

The Bible indicates that the natural man does not understand the spiritual man (see 1 Cor. 2:13-15). This means that our reasoning mind often does not understand our spiritual mind, which is "the mind of Christ" (1 Cor. 2:16). The Holy Spirit reveals things to us when we are ready to handle them. If He revealed everything that's wrong with us at once, we would be crushed, overwhelmed and perhaps give up.

We learn through maturing in Christ that if we trust and obey the Lord when He speaks, God will honor our steps of obedience. We may make mistakes, but God will take our mistakes and turn them around for good. The fact that everything works toward our good does not mean that life will always feel good or that we will enjoy the process. His Word says that He makes "all things work together for good to those who love God, to those called according to his purpose" (Rom. 8:28, *NKJV*), and we can trust His Word.

After serving the Lord for many years, I am totally convinced that it is more difficult to get out of His will than we often think. If we do stray off course, His loving hand will reach out and nudge us back on track.

Relax, Don't Strive

It may be easier than we think to hear the voice of the Lord. We may have to stop trying so hard. God's Word says, "The servant of the Lord must not strive" (2 Tim. 2:24, *KJV*).

Relax and enjoy your relationship with Jesus. The key is to stay submissive to His will and voice.

We certainly need to discern the Lord's voice carefully, but let's not over-spiritualize hearing from God. If God has something to say to us, He knows how to get His point across. It is our responsibility to listen with expectancy and test what we hear. I have also found that if what I am sensing is from God, it often stays with me for a period of time.

Let's continue to listen to the Lord, recognize that He speaks to us because of His wonderful grace, all the while realizing that we are only hearing a part of the whole message. He may want to speak more to us, and He may want to use another method to speak. This keeps us dependent on our growing relationship with Him.

Apply What You've Learned

VERSE TO REMEMBER:

For we know in part.

1 CORINTHIANS 13:9

1. How do we tend to over-spiritualize or make hearing God too difficult?

2. Why do you think God often gives us only a piece of the puzzle?

3. What part does faith play in hearing from God?

13

Visions

While speaking at a church in the South Pacific, I saw a mental picture of a couple walking through a swamp and almost losing each other; however, they managed to come out on the other side totally clean with the sun shining on them as they walked hand in hand. As I shared this with them and prayed, they wept. They had been facing difficult times and wondering if they would survive intact. The mental picture that I had was a vision the Lord gave to me, giving affirmation to this couple that they would make it through the difficult time. Today, they have a ministry that has brought marital healing to couples from various nations of the world.

Throughout the Bible, God has at times spoken to His people through visions. These visions had the various purposes of directing, consoling, confirming, clarifying, instructing, warning or encouraging God's people. The Bible reveals that visions are an important part of the outpouring of the Holy Spirit. "In the last days," God says, "I will pour out my Spirit on all people. Your sons and daughters will prophesy, your young men will see visions, your old men will dream dreams" (Acts 2:17).

Down through the ages, and including the Church today, God gives people visions that clarify their calling or deepen their faith, while giving them a deep assurance from the Lord. Because visions can be symbolic and thus misinterpreted, many in Western Christianity do not take their visions seriously. Others, like the New Age searchers, look for God in the wrong places without discernment and get involved in spiritual phenomena that open them up to the deceptions of Satan.

Just because visions have caused confusion for some in the Body of Christ today does not mean that we should dismiss them. We see countless examples in both the Old and New Testaments of people receiving guidance from God through visions. The Bible tells us that God still speaks through visions, and we must be aware of these "whispers in our ears."

God speaks again and again, though people do not recognize
it. He speaks in dreams, in visions of the night when deep sleep
falls on people as they lie in bed. He whispers in their ear . . .
with his warning. He causes them to change their minds; he
keeps them from pride (Job 33:14-17, *NLT*).

Visions from the Lord give us important information that should
not be ignored.

How can we discern and recognize God's voice in visions? First of
all, it is important for Christians to be rooted and grounded in the
Bible and evaluate every supernatural experience by the Word of God.
We want to be confident that visions are given for the purpose of guidance or protection and that they glorify our Lord Jesus Christ.

In addition, we need to be in communication with other believers
in our local church so that we can receive spiritual discernment for our
visions. Consequently, if you have a vision that you believe is God speaking to you, but you don't understand it, look for someone who may
have the gift of interpretation. Joseph, in the book of Genesis, had this
gift. Look for such an individual who can help you discern the imagery
found within your vision. With this accountability in place, you can
know if a vision is from God.

The Variety in Visions

Paul the apostle was speaking of his own experience when he revealed
to his fellow believers an amazing vision the Lord gave him.

I must go on boasting. Although there is nothing to be gained,
I will go on to visions and revelations from the Lord. I know a
man in Christ who fourteen years ago was caught up to the
third heaven . . . whether in the body or apart from the body I
do not know. . . . He heard inexpressible things (2 Cor. 12:1-4).

Some people believe that the Lord gave Paul this vision of heaven
that could not be described adequately in human language to
strengthen him for his special mission and the exceptional suffering he
would endure.

Unlike dreams, which occur during our sleep, visions are experiences of intense imagery, sound and feeling that occur during the

waking state. There are at least two kinds of visions. One is often referred to as an open vision, which happens when your eyes are open, but you see only the spirit realm instead of your natural surroundings. This is the kind of vision Paul had when he was given the vision of heaven. He was so caught up in the vision that he was unaware of his natural surroundings.

These open visions are external views that are like watching a movie. As with visions, God may or may not give you the interpretation. Never presume to know the meaning. Always allow God to reveal it.

Rick Joyner, a prophet from North Carolina, has had open visions various times. His book *The Final Quest* describes some of these visions and gives encouragement to the Body of Christ.

Another kind of vision you can experience is when you see things "in the spirit." This is a type of impression that the Lord places on your mind and spirit. These impressions or pictures in your mind (mental pictures) are a type of vision the Lord can give to you.

One evening, I saw a vision in the form of a mental picture. The vision was of a particular couple I know, and they were standing in a box. I sensed that I should share it with them. They admitted that they were feeling as if they were restricted in a box. They desperately wanted to move out of the box and into God's destiny for them. My obedience in sharing this vision with them made them realize how much the Lord loves them. It confirmed that He understands how they felt and encouraged them to step out of the confining box they were in.

There have been times when I was looking at someone, but in my spirit I was seeing something concerning that person that my natural eyes did not perceive. Sometimes, the Lord may want us to reveal that information to the person; other times the information has been revealed so that we can pray specifically for the individual.

When my friend LaMarr was a traveling salesman, he had a vision as he sat in a restaurant. In his mind he saw a man, dirty and tired, walking along the road. LaMarr envisioned himself leaving the restaurant and clearing a space on the front seat of his car to prepare for the man to sit there. When LaMarr returned to his car, he moved his briefcase and other papers from the front seat, just as he had seen in his vision. Not far down the road, LaMarr encountered a tired and dirty young man plodding along, and asked him, "Do you need a ride?" With a grateful sigh and nod, the young man took the offer. LaMarr soon learned that the young man had run away from home and was now returning like the prodigal son. As they drove, LaMarr explained the way of salvation and assured the young man he would pray for him. God gave LaMarr the vision to prompt him to reach out to this young man.

Discernment of Visions

Visions are definitely used by God, but we must be cautious and use wisdom and test the spirits, as the Bible instructs us.

> Dear friends, do not believe every spirit, but test the spirits to see whether they are from God, because many false prophets have gone out into the world. This is how you can recognize the Spirit of God: Every spirit that acknowledges that Jesus Christ has come in the flesh is from God, but every spirit that does not acknowledge Jesus is not from God (1 John 4:1-3).

Always examine both the messenger and the message of a vision. Everything real has a counterfeit. If you walk in awe of God's greatness and power and stay in fellowship with fellow believers, you will know the difference.

God gives us visions to reveal and proclaim His loving guidance. If we take the challenge to explore those visions with prayer, we are certain to find the goodness and faithfulness of the Lord in a new way.

Apply What You've Learned

VERSE TO REMEMBER:

"In the last days," God says, "I will pour out my Spirit on all people. Your sons and daughters will prophesy, your young men will see visions."
ACTS 2:17

1. Why do you think many people in Western Christianity do not take their visions seriously?

2. Has God ever spoken to you through a vision?

3. What is the best way to test a vision?

14

Dreams

Danielle had a dream she was back on campus at her alma mater, looking at a syllabus and trying to figure out what she was studying. Her next thought was "Reading Certification." In the morning, she remembered the dream and began making calls to see what would be involved to pursue classes in "Reading Certification." Although she had no previous inclination to go back to school, she suddenly found herself feeling very excited about the possibility. When she shared the dream with her husband, he enthusiastically encouraged her to pursue it.

She also mentioned her dream to her spiritual mentor who said, "God spoke to you in a dream, changed your heart, and your spouse is supportive. Now your heart must bear witness to these circumstances." Danielle is now studying to be a reading specialist. About a month and a half after the dream, her current employment ended quickly and unexpectedly. It was difficult, but having direction for the next step helped Danielle to maintain her purpose and task for what was ahead. God had spoken to her clearly in a dream!

When God speaks to us through visions, we are awake. When He speaks to us through dreams, we are asleep. While our body is at rest, our spirit and mind are quite active. We are "thinking" while sleeping. That's why we can wake up with a song on our lips or wake up with feelings of anger.

Dreams are a valid way that God can speak to us, but are also an area in which people can easily get off balance. Most people dream nightly, and their dreams are not all spiritual dreams. Did you ever wake up from a dream and wonder about its meaning, purpose and origin? Sometimes a dream seems so vivid and real, but you are not sure if the dream's content was God trying to speak to you.

Some dreams may not be God speaking directly, but are our own internal mind and emotions processing our experiences and hopes. While not a direct word from God, they can still be helpful in understanding what we are thinking and feeling. First Corinthians 6:17 tells us that when we are joined to the Lord, our spirit is one spirit with His. I believe that "indirect" dreams are still our spirit processing our life in conjunction with the Holy Spirit.

The Bible has valued the content of dreams for divine revelation in people's lives down through the ages. Sometimes they were dreams of warning or consolation or guidance. In the Old Testament, God spoke to Joseph in a dream, and Joseph interpreted dreams for Pharaoh, as well as for Pharaoh's servants with whom he was in prison (see Gen. 40–41). The Lord spoke to Joseph, the father of Jesus, through a dream, telling him to marry Mary, go to Israel and then to Nazareth in Galilee (see Matt. 1–2). Another time, God warned Joseph in a dream to flee to Egypt with the infant Jesus and cautioned the wise men to go home a different way (see Matt. 2:13).

These dreams had a specific purpose and the message was clear. Those who received the dreams acted in obedience to God. Mary and Joseph fled to Egypt to escape the infanticide ordered by King Herod (see Matt. 2:19-23). The wise men went home on a different route, thus avoiding Herod.

Kinds of Dreams

God spoke to my friend Stan one night in a dream to pray for protection for his friends. During the night, he dreamed there was a fire at their house. After he awakened, he prayed for them. A few days later, he heard that their grill had exploded. He was certain that God had spoken to him in a dream so that he would pray for them. God heard his prayer, and there was no damage to their home.

Emily had a dream about her brother in the Navy. He was dressed up like a fireman and going through a dangerous situation. She woke up and prayed for him. Weeks later, she discovered that he had been in a training exercise in a simulated sinking ship. He was in fireman's gear and said that it was one of the scariest situations he had ever faced.

God sometimes gives dreams to people to console them in life's difficulties. The mother of the Early Church father Augustine was distressed over her then pre-Christian son's immoral lifestyle and begged God for his salvation. The Holy Spirit gave her a dream that showed her worshiping in heaven; and to her great joy, there beside her was her son Augustine. She accepted the dream as a promise that Augustine would come to faith in Jesus, which he later did.

One night, a young lady had a dream that a young woman she was mentoring was very discouraged. The next time she saw her she told her about the dream and asked if everything was okay. The young woman shared that she had struggled with an eating disorder in the past and had been set free, but recently she was being tempted and was struggling again. Her mentor prayed for her and continued to check up on her to help her remain victorious in her Christian walk.

The Promise of Dreams

God promised that we would receive dreams. For most people, they are not daily occurrences, although it seems that there are some people who are more inclined to opening their spiritual eyes and receiving visions and dreams from the Lord than others.

So how can we tell if what we are receiving in a dream is God's voice, the enemy's voice, our internal processing or simply the voice of eating dinner too late? Some dreams are straightforward and clear. We know that they are revealed to clarify something, to instruct us, to warn us or to encourage us. Some dreams are given to us from the Lord only to alert us to pray and intercede.

A pastor friend says that he usually senses if a dream is from God: "Often when I awaken from a dream that seems to have meaning, God's still, small voice is saying, 'That was Me!'" There is an accompanying sense from God that He has spoken.

We must use caution, however, if dreams confuse us. We should not leap to false conclusions about a dream's meaning if it isn't clear. Many, if not most, dreams are figurative and have figurative characters within them and cannot be interpreted concretely. For example, drowning may literally represent stress or feeling overwhelmed about a life situation.

If a dream troubles you, you should discuss it with a trusted mentor, pastor or spiritual director who may be able to give you further insights. There are times when Satan will try to deceive us or cause fear through a dream. If a dream contradicts Scripture, it is clearly demonic.

Dreams from God are given to us when God chooses; we should not search for them and make them our focus. Simply put, God will speak to us in dreams to reveal Himself in a personal way, and the dreams will confirm Scripture, not contradict it.

Some believers write down their dreams to see if they come to pass. If you often dream, may I suggest that you maintain a "dream log." Place it near your bed so that when you wake up in the morning, you can record what you remember. Most of us tend to let the dream escape us if we do not write it down.

Once the dream is recalled and written down, you can begin to pray over it. Counsel with a trusted friend or spiritual overseer, and await its fulfillment. Often these written journals become needed words of encouragement for the future, and often you may come across someone who reminds you of what you dreamt and you suddenly realize that it may be a word of encouragement for him or her.

I encourage you to use discernment, wisdom and balance in hearing God through dreams. If it is God, you will have confirmation in your heart that the Lord is speaking to you or trying to show you something.

Apply What You've Learned

VERSE TO REMEMBER:

I will pour out my Spirit on all people . . .
your old men will dream dreams . . .
JOEL 2:28

1. Has God ever spoken to you through a dream?

2. Describe how a dream, although perhaps not a direct word from God, helped you understand what was going on in your life.

3. Why can people get off-balance when they try to interpret dreams?

15

A Message of Wisdom

When I give birthday gifts to my children, I do not give them presents as a reward for good behavior. I freely and gladly give them gifts because I love them and desire to bless them.

Because God longs for a close relationship with us, He freely gives us spiritual gifts that serve as a means of communication—a divine link between Him and us. Spiritual gifts are not meant to be mysterious. We are to use spiritual gifts to communicate with the Lord and with others. We can hear God through spiritual gifts!

In this chapter, and the following three chapters, we will look at four of these supernatural spiritual gifts from God: a message of wisdom, a message of knowledge, spiritual languages and prophecy. An important point to make about these words of wisdom and knowledge, spiritual languages and prophecy is that they are to be used as tools to build up and encourage one another. As with all the other ways of hearing from God, they need to be used with grace, humility and accountability.

God wants us to understand and use spiritual gifts so that we can be both strengthened and involved in service to others. Paul understood this when he told the church at Rome, "I long to see you so that I may impart to you some spiritual gift to make you strong—that is, that you and I may be mutually encouraged by each other's faith" (Rom. 1:11-12).

The Lord has given His church at least nine different supernatural spiritual gifts:

> Now to each one the manifestation of the Spirit is given for the common good. To one there is given through the Spirit the message of wisdom, to another the message of knowledge by means of the same Spirit, to another faith by the same Spirit, to another gifts of healing by that one Spirit, to another miraculous powers, to another prophecy, to an-

other distinguishing between spirits, to another speaking in different kinds of tongues, and to still another the interpretation of tongues. All these are the work of one and the same Spirit, and he gives them to each one, just as he determines (1 Cor. 2:7-11).

The first detail we notice about these gifts is that they come from the Holy Spirit. Each one of these gifts is supernatural in nature. The gifts allow us to see, know or do things that we are naturally incapable of accomplishing on our own. God gives us these abilities or gifts so that we would have no way of achieving them with our natural abilities. If we use these spiritual gifts in God's way and in His power, not only will we benefit, but others will benefit as well.

We also notice in verse 11 that the Holy Spirit gives gifts to "each one," and He decides who will get which gift. Some believers exercise various spiritual gifts.

The supernatural spiritual gift of "a message of wisdom" is not commonsense wisdom that has been learned through experience. It is not the wisdom that every Christian gains from studying God's Word. It is supernatural wisdom that the Lord gives to us when we need it. It is a gift for all who are faced with a problem beyond their own understanding. The gift of wisdom is the wisdom of God. It is a supernatural impartation; it is not natural. It is received from God through prayer, according to Ephesians 1:17: "I keep asking that the God of our Lord Jesus Christ, the glorious Father, may give you the Spirit of wisdom and revelation, so that you may know him better."

A message of wisdom may be given to encourage someone to trust God more, or pray with greater faith or embrace a deeper spiritual life. Even a young Christian may have the revelation gift of the word of wisdom despite the fact that he has very little biblical wisdom from studying God's Word.

Solomon received wisdom from God, but we only have a record of his receiving a word of wisdom or a special revelation for a special problem a couple of times. In 1 Kings 3, Solomon needed supernatural wisdom when two women both claimed a baby after one of their babies had been smothered to death during the night. The Spirit of God showed Solomon to call for a sword. He said that he would divide the live baby between the two women; but one of the mothers cried out to save the baby's life. Solomon knew that this woman was the baby's rightful mother. Solomon had prayed and asked for wisdom from the Lord, which was then given by the Spirit for that specific problem.

Joseph, through supernatural wisdom from God, gave Pharaoh insights to govern Egypt properly in order to prepare for the coming famine.

Paul was exercising a supernatural gift of a message of wisdom when he gave the commander of the ship to Rome guidance regarding navigation (see Acts 27).

There are times when I am called upon as a consultant that I feel "out of my league," but again and again the Lord gives me supernatural wisdom to pass on to ministry leaders. This wisdom I have not learned through trial and error. It comes from the Lord through a supernatural message of wisdom that allows me to speak appropriate truth at the right time.

Likewise, one of my associates, who is a marriage counselor, is amazed at times when the Lord gives him supernatural wisdom that brings life and healing to marriages. The Lord drops this gift of wisdom into his spirit and he passes it on to those he is counseling. The gift of wisdom will provide them with simple, practical solutions in the midst of conflict.

A supernatural message of wisdom is one of the many ways in which the Lord speaks to us. He may give you a supernatural message of wisdom to solve a problem you are going through by allowing you to know the next steps to take. Or the Lord may give you a supernatural message of wisdom to help someone else by providing practical solutions for him or her. In addition, He may give someone else a supernatural message of wisdom to help you so that you can know God's best in a given situation.

Remember, the gift of wisdom is the wisdom of God. It is a supernatural impartation; it is not natural. You can't earn it. It is received from God through prayer (see Eph. 1:17) and involves being led by the Holy Spirit to act appropriately to apply that impartation of wisdom. In the next chapter, we will look at the supernatural gift of knowledge.

Apply What You've Learned

VERSE TO REMEMBER:

Now to each one the manifestation of the Spirit is given for the common good. To one there is given through the Spirit the message of wisdom.
1 CORINTHIANS 12:4

1. Why does God give us spiritual gifts?

2. Did you ever discern something because God supernaturally revealed it to you? How did you know the wisdom was from God?

3. Tell of a time when God has spoken to you through a message of wisdom.

16

A Message of Knowledge

On their honeymoon at Disney World, a young couple visited the Epcot Center. At the Mongolian exhibit, God began to reveal Himself in a very special way. They realized that God was speaking to them about the nation of Mongolia. "We'll do whatever You want us to do" was their immediate prayer. They kept this revelation alive in their hearts for about three years without telling anyone about it. One day, an intercessor friend said to them, "Does the word 'Mongolia' mean anything to you?" They were stunned with this message of knowledge from the Lord. Their friend had no prior knowledge of their heart for Mongolia. The couple received training and soon was sent out by their church, along with a team, to Mongolia.

A message of knowledge is a supernatural spiritual gift from the Lord that allows us to discover information that we have not had prior access to or been aware of by any natural means. It is a message that provides particular information that is needed by a believer or by the church body at a particular time. It may provide direction, or it may provide information on possible traps or danger.

For example, in Acts 5, Peter received a message of knowledge about Ananias and Sapphira's deception in giving a gift to the church, and the results were quite sobering. They both died in the midst of their deception! God got the instant attention of the entire church!

Many times the Lord uses various spiritual gifts to get our attention. One time, God used the gift of a message of knowledge to speak to a wayward young man for whom I was praying. This young man had grown up in a Christian home but was now backslidden and had a secret sin in his life: he was addicted to alcohol. Even though he had recently made a commitment to return to the Lord, he was still struggling with a lack of peace in his life. He did not tell me about his alcohol problem.

We talked for some time, and then I suggested that we spend time praying together. As soon as I closed my eyes and began to pray, I saw a clear mental picture of a liberty bell. It did not make sense to me, but I asked him if a liberty bell meant anything to him.

He said that it made no sense to him at all. Then he suddenly remembered something. "Come to think of it," he said, "I have continued to drink alcohol in secret and have given the impression that I am free from alcohol. There is a liberty bell on the bottle that I am now drinking."

The Lord showed me a liberty bell, a supernatural gift of knowledge that I had no prior information about, to jolt his thinking about an area of secret sin in his life. God got his attention, and today, he is free from his addiction to alcohol.

In his book *The Supernatural Power of a Transformed Mind*, Bill Johnson tells the story of his associate, Kris, who was traveling on a flight seated next to a six-foot-four man with a spike coming out of his chin and a tattoo of a satanic head. Kris, who operates strongly in the gifts of the Spirit, received revelation about John and soon was speaking into his life. "Your father abandoned you. You look tough, but you really are a mama's boy. You love children and you feel like you are supposed to work with orphans." John, a bass player for a heavy metal band, was shocked by the accuracy of Kris's words. John's life changed because he realized God knew the secrets of his heart. A word of knowledge brings revelation to a person at the right moment to capture someone's immediate attention.

Another time, Bill and an associate, Mike, were standing in line at a Starbucks in the airport. Bill was focused on receiving his steaming cup of coffee when he noticed that Mike was praying for the cashier. Mike told Bill later that he had seen a spirit of suicide on the cashier, and he had prayed to break that power. She told him, "God sent you in here today."[1]

Revelation Gifts that Often Work Together

A message of wisdom that we looked at in the last chapter frequently works interactively with the revelation gift of a message of knowledge. A message of wisdom brings together knowledge that already exists and gives direction to it so that God can be heard clearly.

Acts 9:10-16 is a good example of a message of knowledge and a message of wisdom working together. Here, Jesus appeared to Ananias (not the Ananias of Acts 5) in a vision and told him to go to a certain street and find Saul of Tarsus. God told Ananias that Saul was praying, and that he had received a vision in which he saw a man named Ananias coming in and laying hands on him. This was a message of knowledge.

After this, Ananias expressed his concerns regarding Saul. In response, Jesus told Ananias to go to Saul because he was a chosen vessel to bear God's name to the Gentiles, and God would show him the things he must suffer. This part of the passage was a word of wisdom. Jesus revealed to Ananias a word of wisdom concerning His divine purpose for Saul, and so we see the two gifts working together.

In the next chapter, we will look at another supernatural gift from the Lord that is sometimes misunderstood—spiritual languages.

Apply What You've Learned

VERSE TO REMEMBER:

Now to each one the manifestation of the Spirit is given for the common good. To one there is given through the Spirit . . . the message of knowledge.
1 CORINTHIANS 12:7-8

1. Have you ever received a message of knowledge that changed your direction in life?

2. Describe any time you have received a message of knowledge for another person.

3. How can God speak through both a message of wisdom and knowledge?

Note
1. Bill Johnson, *The Supernatural Power of a Transformed Mind* (Shippensburg, PA: Destiny Image Publishers, Inc., 2005), pp. 65-67, 113.

17

Spiritual Languages

A housewife awoke one night, startled by the sound of screeching tires. She ran to the window and realized there was no one in sight. With the Holy Spirit urging her, she spent some time praying in the Spirit in her spiritual language and then drifted off to sleep.[1] A few days later, one of her closest friends phoned her and said, "You'll never guess what happened to us!" She went on to describe a near accident in which the tires screeched and her family was miraculously spared. She knew that angels must have been sent from the throne room of God. The almost fatal accident happened at exactly the same time this faithful housewife was praying in the Spirit!

The Bible says that we pray in two ways—with our mind and with our spirit. Both are needed, and both are under the influence of the Holy Spirit, according to 1 Corinthians 14:14:

> For if I pray in a tongue, my spirit prays, but my mind is unfruitful. So what shall I do? I will pray with my spirit, but I will also pray with my mind.

When the housewife prayed in the Spirit, she didn't know exactly what she was praying for, but her spirit was praying directly to the Father without having to accept the limitations of her human intellect. God knew what she was saying, and I believe He answered those prayers in the middle of the night, keeping her friend's family safe.

The gift of "spiritual languages," or "tongues," is sometimes controversial in today's church.[2] Nevertheless, many believers have received this gift and exercise it in their personal conversations with God as they pray for situations they may not know how to pray for in their natural language, or as they enter into times of worship and praise.

The Bible says that our spiritual language magnifies God (see Acts 10:46). This personal prayer language is understood by God because it is our spirit speaking to God. Speaking in our spiritual language is a direct line of communication between us and God.

Jack Hayford says that the biblical expression of tongues often "conjures up strange images in people's minds because they have images of uncontrolled speech or weird gibberish." Hayford maintains that to use the expression "spiritual language" is a more easily accepted description of tongues speaking and is precisely biblical.

The expression "spiritual language" is derived from such references where speaking or singing with tongues is described. The phrases "filled with the Spirit" and "praying . . . in the Spirit" are the same in the biblical Greek—*en pneumati*. This phrase literally means, "in the spiritual realm and with the Holy Spirit's aid." Of course, using the word "spiritual" for this prayer language isn't to suggest that spoken prayer or praise in one's native language is unspiritual or semispiritual. Each form of prayer is at a different dimension, and neither should be described as "less than." How can the Grand Canyon and the Swiss Alps be compared? It's impossible and unnecessary to do so. Rather, be it languages we employ or creation we behold, let us all be humbled before all manifestations of His Majesty's glory. Let us rise together to praise the Creator of all things. To do so is to be open to experiencing the enjoyment and the blessing available in exploring the dimensions to which each realm invites us.[3]

Sometimes the Lord gives individuals messages in a language they have not learned in order to speak to others about the goodness of God in a public setting.

The Bible describes this kind of spiritual language in Acts 2:4-12:

All of them were filled with the Holy Spirit and began to speak in other tongues as the Spirit enabled them. Now there were staying in Jerusalem God-fearing Jews from every nation under heaven. When they heard this sound, a crowd came together in bewilderment, because each one heard them speaking in his own language. Utterly amazed, they asked: "Are not all these men who are speaking Galileans? *Then how is it that each of us hears them in his own native language?* . . . we hear them declaring the wonders of God in our own tongues!" Amazed and perplexed, they asked one another, "What does this mean?" (emphasis added).

This miracle of everyone hearing the Lord speak through the apostles and believers in their own language opened the door for Peter to preach the gospel, and 3,000 people came to faith in Christ that day.

My colleague Steve and his wife, Mary, were ministering at a church in Curaçao, an island off the north coast of Venezuela. It was a very hot Sunday afternoon under a tiki hut, where they had just finished a church picnic. Steve and Mary offered to pray for the sick earlier that morning, so a line began to form. Before they knew it, they were praying for several hours, and God was touching people and bringing healing to many. Most people in Curaçao speak four languages: Dutch, Spanish, English and Papiamento (a native dialect). Of course, Steve and Mary were praying in English. A young man came forward and shared his physical need, and Steve began to pray in his spiritual language. Mary was praying in English. After the prayer, the young man looked at Steve with a question on his face and stated, "I didn't know you spoke Papiamento."

"I don't" was Steve's reply.

"But you spoke it perfectly when you were praying."

"Really? What did I pray?" Steve asked.

The young man said, "You spoke for God and told me what I was to do. In fact, I didn't believe that you knew my language, so I asked the Holy Spirit to have you say it again, and you spoke the same phrase a second time!"

About this incident, Steve said, "Did I speak in Papiamento or did the young man hear me pray in his language? I don't know, but either way, it was a miracle, and the Father spoke a message to His son!"

Jack Hayford, in his book *The Beauty of Spiritual Language*, tells the story of sitting on an airplane talking to a businessman who mentioned his Native American ancestry. The Lord then prompted Jack to ask the man if he could speak a few words of his spiritual language (tongues). The man was agreeable, and Jack spoke aloud a few phrases. The man said it indeed was his tribal language, and Jack was speaking about a Light that had come to the world. Jack, obviously, had never learned this tribal language, but the Lord gave it to him supernaturally. Jack's spiritual language opened the door for him to share the Light of the gospel with the businessman.[4]

Ron Myer, my associate in ministry for 20 years, was praying in his spiritual language during a prayer time before a church service. A visiting African pastor told Ron later that he was speaking fluently in his native language. Ron had never learned the African language, but the Lord gave it to him supernaturally.

God wants us to have and use the gift of spiritual languages so that we may be encouraged and also be a blessing to others. We need to exercise this gift so that it can be used to build us up spiritually to give us supernatural strength and ability to be effective in our Christian life.

We should "eagerly desire spiritual gifts" (1 Cor. 14:1). All of the gifts are given to serve others; hence, no one can claim superiority about any one spiritual gift. All gifts have the purpose of glorifying Christ and benefiting others so that we can all hear from God more clearly. God gives you spiritual gifts so that you can effectively help your brothers and sisters in Christ hear from heaven and so that you might minister effectively to those who do not yet know Jesus.

Apply What You've Learned

VERSE TO REMEMBER:

Now to each one the manifestation of the Spirit is given for the common good. To one there is given through the Spirit . . . speaking in different kinds of tongues.
1 CORINTHIANS 12:4

1. Explain how someone can pray with his mind and with his spirit.

2. Have you ever heard God speak through a spiritual language? If so, how?

3. If you use a personal prayer language, how does your spiritual language glorify God?

Notes
1. Often called "speaking in tongues." In this chapter, we explain why the term "spiritual languages" is preferred.
2. For more about speaking in tongues, read Larry Kreider's booklet *How to be Filled with the Holy Spirit* (Lititz, PA: House to House Publications, 2007) or *Biblical Foundation Series: Book # 3, New Testament Baptisms* (Lititz, PA: House to House Publications, 2002).
3. Jack Hayford, *The Beauty of Spiritual Language* (Nashville, TN: Thomas Nelson, Inc., 1992), p. 92.
4. Ibid., pp. 199-200.

18

Prophecy

When the Lord speaks a message through one person for the benefit of another, it is often called a prophecy. When a prophetic message is given, it is for the purpose of knowing that God will speak directly to you. The Lord will reveal to you that the prophetic word given is a personal message from heaven, for the Bible says, "Everyone who prophesies speaks to men for their strengthening, encouragement and comfort" (Acts 11:28). In the Old Testament, prophecy was often given to bring judgment, but in the New Testament, it is for strengthening, encouraging and comforting believers.

Sometimes prophecy is foretelling a future event, such as the prophecy Agabus the prophet gave in the book of Acts when he predicted a famine (see Acts 11:27-28); while at other times it can be a message of encouragement for God's people (see 1 Cor. 14:3).

God also wants His people to receive a current revelation from Him so that we know what He is saying and doing in the world today. In chapter 1, we described God's Word as both *logos* and *rhema*. Prophecy is a *rhema* word that sometimes clarifies and emphasizes God's already revealed heart, mind and plans in His *logos* word. It will never conflict with the written word; in fact, it often makes the Bible come alive to us.

When God says something prophetically about you, He is speaking out and releasing your potential. God is supernatural, and as Christians, we must by definition be supernatural as well. A pastor I know from Germany often says, "God wants us to be naturally supernatural, and supernaturally natural." People today are hungry for the supernatural; you only have to look at the popular books and movies of our day to see this theme of supernatural events or people using supernatural powers. I believe that God places this desire for the supernatural in us, yet the enemy is quick to take advantage and produces a counterfeit that draws people away from God, rather than closer to Him.

God Speaks Through Others

We may receive a prophecy directly for us, or the Lord may speak to us through a prophecy given by someone else for us. Dr. Bill Hamon defines prophecy as:

> [Prophecy is] God communicating His thoughts and intents to mankind. When a true prophecy is given, the Holy Spirit inspires someone to communicate God's pure and exact words to the individual or group for whom they are intended. It is delivered without any additions or subtractions by the one prophesying, including any applications or interpretations suggested by the one speaking. To be most effective, it must also be delivered in God's timing and with the proper spirit or attitude.[1]

The New Testament prophets revealed Jesus through their words of encouragement and insights on coming events, and it is the model for the Church today. The Bible gives many examples of prophecies that were spoken to give direction to the people of God.

Agabus, a prophet mentioned in the book of Acts, prophesied that if Paul went to Jerusalem, he would be bound and delivered to the Gentiles. It happened just as he foretold—Paul was arrested and tried in Jerusalem (see Acts 21-22). Timothy received a spiritual gift through a prophetic message when the elders laid their hands on him and prayed for him (see 1 Tim. 4:14). Paul told Timothy to wage warfare with prophetic words given to him. "Timothy, my son, I give you this instruction in keeping with the prophecies once made about you, so that by following them you may fight the good fight" (1 Tim. 1:18).

Many times, prophecies are confirmations of those things the Lord has already spoken to us in our heart. At other times, the Lord may use prophecy to give us clear direction for our life. Both ways, the prophecy must be in line with the Word of God, and our spirits must affirm it.

All prophecy needs to be tested. "Do not put out the Spirit's fire; do not treat prophecies with contempt. Test everything. Hold on to the good" (1 Thess. 5:19-22). Testing a prophecy may mean that we go to our pastor or other trusted Christian leader to present it to them and ask for their input. Additionally, all prophecy must be tested by Scripture. If it does not line up with what we read in Scripture, do not receive it.

According to God's Timing

We must especially test a prophetic word for timing. It may be for today, or it may be for 10 years down the road. We must be careful not to assume that we know immediately what every personal prophecy means. I learned this the hard way.

Several years ago, I had two prophetic messages spoken over me about being called to minister to young people, just as I did more than two decades ago. One prophetic message came from a pastor in Oregon, and the other came from a pastor in New Zealand. I assumed from receiving these two nearly identical prophecies that I was to start a youth ministry, so I did. I began meeting with about 35 youth every week in my hometown.

Shortly thereafter, the Lord also brought me into a relationship with some young leaders who had started a weekly Tuesday Bible study (TBS). As our friendship grew, these leaders started to look to me as one of their spiritual advisors for their fledgling group. While the youth ministry I had started was declining, the TBS youth ministry had grown to more than 1,000 young people.

I finally realized that I had missed God's timing; He never wanted me to start a new youth ministry. He called me, however, to be a mentor to these young leaders. If I had waited to see what God was going to do with TBS, I wouldn't have started the other youth ministry. Timing is always a critical part of seeing a prophetic word come to pass. Misperceiving the timing for prophetic words or attempting to fulfill a prophetic word yourself are the most common errors people make in processing prophecy.

Confirmed in the Heart

Often we are tempted to add to the prophetic word. This usually brings confusion (see John 21:23). A friend told me of a prophetic word spoken over him and his wife that said, "I see children." Afterward, people quickly speculated that they would soon be pregnant because they already had two children. The word never said "pregnancy," and later they saw how they had mentored a teenage mother in their home, like a "daughter."

If somebody tells you through a prophetic word to go to the mission field, please don't quit your job unless you know that God has also spoken this same word to you and it is confirmed by other ways the Lord speaks to you—His peace; circumstances; His still, small voice, for example. I've seen people get into awful problems by trying to run their life based on what other people told them was a prophetic message from God.

If the prophecy you receive doesn't bear agreement in your heart, you will know it by a lack of peace in your spirit. Something tells you that things just are not quite right.

There are a lot of well-meaning people who think they are hearing from God for others, but the truth is, they are not. If someone prophesies something to you that is not already in your heart, then I suggest you write down the words that are spoken over you and wait for the Lord to reveal to you whether or not the words are from Him. If it is from God, He will confirm it in other ways and bring His Word to pass in your life.

God Speaks Through You

The Lord desires to place His words in our mouths and speak through us prophetically to others. Jesus promises to "give you words and wisdom that none of your adversaries will be able to resist or contradict" (Luke 21:15). If the Lord speaks a message in your spirit that you believe is a true prophecy for someone else, don't be presumptuous when giving it to the individual. If possible, have the individual's spiritual leaders involved in this process so that they can help the person discern the meaning of the prophecy.

I would also encourage you to share the word of prophecy in the form of a question. In other words, rather than a "thus saith the Lord," as often as possible begin by saying, "Could the Lord be saying . . . ?" or "Tell me if your spirit resonates with the word that is on my heart."

God wants us to be encouraged with prophecies that help us know Him better. Remember, prophecy is just one of the ways that God speaks to us and should not be used exclusively to hear from

God. Nevertheless, let's continue to seek Him and keep our hearts open as He speaks prophetic words that refresh our walk with Him.

Apply What You've Learned

VERSE TO REMEMBER:

Everyone who prophesies speaks to men for their strengthening, encouragement and comfort.

ACTS 11:28

1. How can you determine if a prophecy spoken over you is true or not?

2. Why is timing so important for prophetic words?

3. Tell of any time the Lord gave a prophecy to you or for someone else and you knew it was God speaking clearly.

Note
1. Dr. Bill Hamon, *Prophets and Personal Prophecy* (Shippensburg, PA: Destiny Image, 1987), p. 29.

Section Four

OBSERVATION

19

Circumstances

I was in Nairobi, Kenya, several years ago when terrorists bombed the U.S. Embassy, killing nearly 1,000 people. That morning, Diane Omondi, the wife of the pastor who was sponsoring the leadership training at which I was teaching, planned to go to the embassy to help process a visa for a friend. Through a set of circumstances at the last minute, it did not work out for her to go.

Had she gone, Diane might have been in the U.S. Embassy when the bomb exploded. In this instance, the Lord used a "closed door" circumstance to protect one of His children. The Bible says that God can open a door or close it at will: "These are the words of the Holy One, the True One, He Who has the key of David, Who opens and no one shall shut, Who shuts and no one shall open" (Rev. 3:7, *AMP*).

Paul saw God open a door of opportunity for him and believed it was the Lord directing him through the providential circumstances. "After I go through Macedonia, I will come to you. . . . I hope to spend some time with you, if the Lord permits. But I will stay on at Ephesus until Pentecost, because a great door for effective work has opened to me, and there are many who oppose me" (1 Cor. 16:5-9).

The Lord clearly opened a door for Paul in Ephesus. The circumstances lined up with the Word of God and with the peace of God, and although Paul faced many adversaries, he knew that the Lord wanted him to stay in Ephesus.

We must be aware that not every open door means we should go running through it. The key to walking through an open door is to know without a doubt the Lord has opened it. The Holy Spirit must be speaking to us before we make a move to walk in a new direction.

Circumstances that seemingly reveal open doors may not necessarily be the Lord speaking to us to move in a particular direction. Focusing only on the circumstances can be misleading. For example, a college student may receive a large scholarship to attend a particular university, but he must know that God is in it or he may make the wrong choice just because the circumstances are favorable.

Before we walk through an open door, we must believe that it is God who is speaking to us within the circumstances, have the peace of God about it and know that it does not conflict with God's Word.

Timing

Sometimes we can be so sure that something is God's will for us, but God does not open up the door because it is not the right timing. If you feel this way, it is best to let the desire die. If it is really from God, He will resurrect it (bring it back to life) in the future when the timing is right.

We have counseled countless young men and women who were sure the Lord had shown them the person they were to marry, but the other person wasn't getting the same message. Our advice is to let the desire die for now, and if the Lord has really spoken it to you, it will happen sometime in the future. We all hear from God "in part" (1 Cor. 13:9) and must recognize that we do not always hear clearly.

If you believe that the Lord wants you to buy a certain house or car, and it is not available, or you do not have the financial means, either you have missed the timing or it is not the Lord's answer for you. Timing is especially critical when it comes to circumstances.

Brian and a young woman were friends when Brian felt called to marry her. She, however, was preparing to go with a church planting team to Scotland. It was apparent to Brian that the timing was not right, so he waited for a year and a half until Janet returned. After her return from missionary service, he asked her to marry him, and she said yes. Although God spoke to Brian much earlier about marrying Janet, the timing had to be right.

You may have been given the right direction from the Lord, but the timing is wrong as you try to fulfill it. Moses had the right vision from the Lord (deliver the Lord's people from the slavery of the Egyptians). The only problem was that he initially missed the timing of God (by 40 years!) when he killed an Egyptian.

A friend recently shared how God continues to work through circumstances and timing in his marriage relationship to help them make godly decisions. He told me that he often gets a new a vision from God for their lives and is ready to move on that vision because he believes that God is opening the door of circumstances. His wife, on the other hand, does not always immediately see the open door. When she does, the timing has always been correct. Together, they can hear God to make the right decision.

Open Doors

If the Lord is asking you to do something, He will make it clear. The biblical prophet Jeremiah received a message from the Lord to buy a field, but he needed confirmation from his cousin. His cousin came to visit him in prison and told him the land was available for purchase (see Jer. 32:6-8). After the circumstances lined up, Jeremiah knew that the message was a sure word from the Lord.

If we are not sure about an open door, we can trust God to speak within the circumstances in which we currently find ourselves. Recently, I talked with two high school students who were wondering what the Lord was calling them to do. Then they realized that God had them in school for a reason—to be used exactly where they were. They focused on school in a new way, and they began inviting their school friends to church every week. Many of the young people responded. School was the circumstance providing open doors for their ministry.

In Acts 27, Paul was shipwrecked on the island of Malta. This shipwreck circumstance led to Paul's three-month stay on the island, resulting in many of the people opening up to the saving message of the gospel.

Changed Circumstances

If we believe that God wants us to move ahead in a certain direction, but the circumstances do not match God's revealed will, He may be calling us to prayer, spiritual warfare and action to see the circumstance change.

In 1 Kings 18, God showed Elijah that He would send rain to end a drought. Elijah prayed for the rain, but it did not come. Seven times Elijah sent his servant to look at the sky to see if rain clouds were forming. No rain! But Elijah was persistent in his prayer. Rather than get discouraged, he simply kept on praying until he saw evidence of the answer to his prayer.

Elijah prayed earnestly because he wanted to participate in the means by which God achieves His purposes. He believed that God would send rain because God had promised it, but Elijah had to keep praying until the circumstances changed. The circumstances, in fact, did change. It rained just as God said it would, but only after Elijah resolutely prayed and persevered for the change.

Stepping Out

Bible teacher Joyce Meyer once said, "Sometimes the only way to discover God's will is to practice what I call 'stepping out and finding out.' If I have prayed about a situation and don't seem to know what I should do, I take a step of faith. . . . Some doors will never open unless we take a step toward them."[1]

In the book of Acts, and in 1 Corinthians 16, Paul, Silas and Barnabas did not sit and wait for an angel to appear or a vision to be given them while praying for direction. They took steps in the direction they felt was correct. Many times God did open the door, but there were times when He closed the door. This did not discourage them. They were not afraid of "missing God." They were men of faith and action who were willing to take a risk. They also knew when to back off quickly when it became evident that God was not permitting them to follow the plan they were pursuing.

Today, we, too, can hear God's voice through circumstances as He opens and closes doors of opportunity. The key is to always be led by the Holy Spirit, not by the circumstances themselves. The Spirit may capture our attention by a combination of factors that include open-door circumstances and a word from a friend. Other times He could speak through circumstances that lead us to Scripture that confirms the circumstances. God speaks to our individual need, and we will sense when He has spoken.

Apply What You've Learned

VERSE TO REMEMBER:

Because a great door for effective work has opened to me.
1 CORINTHIANS 16:9

1. Why are favorable conditions not always open doors to walk through?

2. Describe a time when the circumstances were right but the timing was off in your hearing from God.

3. Will God change the circumstances when we pray? How?

Note
1. Joyce Meyer, *How to Hear from God* (New York: Time Warner Book Group, 2003), p. 176.

20

Natural Things

I love to go to the ocean. I experience the Lord's majestic power at the seashore as I see an ocean that is so amazingly massive and yet its mighty roaring waves stop at a certain place because God has commanded them to go no farther. When sitting by the ocean, I gain great strength as I watch the pounding waves. They speak to me of the vast strength and awesome power of the Lord. Perhaps you took notice of this already, but Jesus often taught on or beside a body of water.

I also love the mountains, where I experience God's majesty in the breathtaking views across a valley or the snow-capped peaks in the distance. God speaks to me through the nature of this world He has created. There is a deep "knowing within" that God is making Himself known to me through the masterpieces of His creation.

The Bible confirms that God reveals Himself through nature. "The heavens declare the glory of God; the skies proclaim the work of his hands" (Ps. 19:1). Psalm 29:3-8 says:

> The voice of the LORD is over the waters; the God of glory thunders. . . . The voice of the LORD is powerful; the voice of the LORD is majestic. The voice of the LORD breaks the cedars. . . . The voice of the LORD strikes with flashes of lightning. The voice of the LORD shakes the desert.

In nature, we discover a nonstop manifestation of God. Nature sends a clear signal that everyone can receive.

God told Abraham to look at the stars to get a vision of his future family. The vast starry sky symbolized the countless ancestors that God promised He would give Abraham (see Gen. 15:5).

From the beginning of creation, God has shown what His eternal power and character are like by all that He has made (see Rom. 1:20). Even those who are not living in the will of God can perceive right from wrong and instinctively know that God exists, because nature itself testifies of His existence. That's why people cannot claim ignorance of God as an excuse for refusing to honor Him. Atheists will some day stand before the Lord and realize that God spoke through His handiwork as they ignored this revelation in nature (see Rom. 1:21).

It was through the very intricate design of God's handiwork in the human body that God spoke to the American writer Whittaker Chambers when he was still an atheist. He was observing his infant daughter and was struck by the fact that such an exquisite creature was not an accident or a freak of nature. He recalls in his autobiography:

My eye came to rest on the delicate convolutions of her ear— those intricate, perfect ears. The thought passed through my mind: "No, those ears were not created by any chance coming together of atoms in nature. They could have been created only by immense design."[1]

God revealed Himself clearly in the design of a child. Mr. Chambers could not ignore God's voice speaking to him.

While on this earth, Jesus often used nature to teach spiritual lessons so that we could more clearly understand how God communicates with mankind. Jesus told us to consider the lilies of the field (see Matt. 6:28) and the ravens of the air (see Luke 12:24). Meditating on how God adorns the fields and provides for the birds will remind us that if He cares so completely for nature, then He cares even more deeply for mankind whom He made in His own image.

Another time, Jesus told a parable of a budding fig tree, giving proof that summer was near, to speak symbolically of the "budding" of God's kingdom that begins in the hearts of those who are receptive. Those who trust in God's Word will bear the fruit of His kingdom (see Matt. 24:32-33). Again, God was speaking to mankind through a natural sign to make His words easier to understand.

When Moses led the children of Israel out of Egypt, God revealed His guiding presence in the form of a cloud by day, and by a pillar of fire by night (see Exod. 13:21-22). A cloud settled down on the tabernacle, filling it with God's glory (see Exod. 40:34-35). The same thing happened when Solomon finished building the Temple (see 1 Kings 8:11-13). The cloud symbolized the glory of God's majesty and presence that filled the Temple. God was speaking His blessing as He took up residence in the Temple.

Through the observation of life situations and natural phenomena, the Lord often speaks a lesson or insight. Learning to observe and listen for God to speak through nature is a very fruitful way to learn from God.

Jana, a new believer, was traveling to work one morning in heavy Dallas traffic when she noticed a tiny clip of a rainbow in the sky. It was a dull, cloudy day, but this little piece of rainbow hovered above timidly. Although she enjoyed it, she questioned, "Lord, this reminds me of Your promises. Are they really still true, or just a little true? Why don't I ever see big, beautiful rainbows anymore?" The very next morning, Jana turned to get on the freeway, and right over a lake was the biggest, most intense rainbow she had ever seen stretched all the way across the horizon! It was as if God said, "Yes, Jana, I love you, and yes, My promises are true!" God's speaking through nature in this way caused Jana to realize that God cared about her personally.

Every morning the sun comes up, and every evening it goes down. The stars come out in the sky, and the universe remains in order as a reminder that God is watching over us each day. He keeps the planets in place, broadcasting His unfathomable power and glory as all the planets in the solar system travel along God's predetermined orbit.

If He can hold the sun and the stars in place, we can be assured He is able to keep our lives in order too. While traveling in northern Scotland, I experienced the wonder of its pristine starry sky. (Since the north of Scotland suffers less than other developed countries from urban glare, the stars are quite magnificent.) I felt so close to the Lord as I again experienced God's enormity and love. The Lord comforted and encouraged me through His natural creation. I knew without a doubt that God held the world in His hand and, no matter what was wrong in the world, He would sustain me because He is the Creator.

Where I live in Pennsylvania, the deciduous trees stretch their bare limbs to the sky, revealing a stark, surreal look in the wintertime. Yet these same trees come back to life each spring as their leaves bud once again and they fill out with fresh, beautiful foliage. It's a reminder that God will bring our lives back to full bloom even if we feel that our present circumstances are dismal.

Along with the many other ways God speaks, look for God to speak through His creation. It is a clear signal that He cares for you.

Apply What You've Learned

VERSE TO REMEMBER:

The heavens declare the glory of God; the skies proclaim the work of his hands.

PSALM 19:1

1. How does God show His character through what He has made in nature?
2. How can people perceive right from wrong through nature?
3. How has God revealed Himself to you through nature?

Note
1. Whittaker Chambers, *Witness* (Washington, D.C.: Regnery Publishing, 1987), p. 15.

21

Signs

Many years ago, there was a popular song on the radio with the lyric, "Signs, signs, everywhere a sign . . ." Truly, there are signs everywhere in our world. One sign I often look for when driving is the one along the highway that confirms the direction I am traveling. Signs reveal information, sometimes desired and sometimes undesired.

A few years ago, Florida motorists received some tongue-in-cheek messages "signed" by God in the form of a billboard campaign. Large signs were emblazoned with short messages saying things like:

"We need to talk."—God.
"I don't question *your* existence."
"Will the road you're on get you to My place?"
"Keep taking My name in vain and I'll make rush hour longer."
"Have you read My #1 bestseller? There will be a test."

These signs endeavored to get people to reconsider that God still speaks today and has timeless truth to offer mankind. I don't know if God actually spoke to anyone's heart through those roadside signs, but I'd like to think that He did. I believe that God loves to grab our attention and speak to us in unexpected ways.

Sometimes, if we are having trouble hearing from God, we may attempt to put God to the test, so to speak, to make sure that He is speaking to us. This kind of attempt to hear God's voice by asking for a specific sign is often called "laying out a fleece." We get this term from Gideon's experience in the Bible.

In the book of Judges (see 6:36-40), we read that Gideon desired a sign from God and laid out a wool fleece before the Lord for confirmation and direction. If dew appeared only on the fleece and not on the ground, Gideon would know that God had spoken. It happened! But Gideon was still unsure and asked the Lord to do the reverse of the sign to fully prove it. This time God made the fleece dry and the ground covered with dew. By now Gideon was quite sure this was really God speaking to him.

I believe this shows that unless the sign is supernatural and direct, it's best to look at signs as a confirmation of other forms of hearing to be sure that we are receiving clear direction from the Lord. When God is trying to get a message to us, He often uses multiple means at once. If you have prophetic words, circumstances and Scripture working together, then a sign of some sort may come as confirmation.

Signs God Has Used in the Past

Without a doubt, God used signs to speak dramatically throughout the history of mankind. In Genesis, He sent a well-known sign that took the form of a rainbow. This sign was a promise of God's covenant between Himself and every living creature on Earth. God said:

> This is the sign of the covenant I am making between me and you and every living creature with you, a covenant for all generations to come: I have set my rainbow in the clouds, and it will be the sign of the covenant between me and the earth. Whenever I bring clouds over the earth and the rainbow appears in the clouds, I will remember my covenant between me and you and all living creatures of every kind (Gen. 9:12-15).

On another occasion, God sent a supernatural sign that stopped time. The sun stood still for a day so that the Israelites could fight and win a battle. Only God could manage such a feat, causing the Israelites to recognize that God was on their side.

> On the day the Lord gave the Amorites over to Israel, Joshua said to the Lord in the presence of Israel: "O sun, stand still over Gibeon, O moon, over the Valley of Aijalon." So the sun stood still, and the moon stopped, till the nation avenged itself on its enemies! (Josh. 10:12-14).

Caution About Hearing God Through Signs

Of all the ways in which God speaks, signs may be one of the easiest to misinterpret. If you really want something badly, it's easy to think that just about anything is a sign of God's approval. We should use caution and not become dependent on these kinds of signs to hear from God, because they are rather unusual ways to confirm His will. Additionally, we should probably not depend on a sign to be the sole factor in making a decision; however, it is clear that the Lord will sometimes honor and answer our request for a sign.

Someone once said that our goal should "not be to improve our testing of God's will, but to improve our relationship with God." God really wants a relationship with us that is strong enough for us to understand what He is saying without "testing" Him. We can become spiritually lazy in looking for signs, when we should be learning to listen to and discern God's voice. If we learn to hear His Spirit's voice, we will not need to set up a complicated test to see if it is really Him speaking.

There are times when God does allow Himself to be tested. I believe He understands that there are times when we need and desire proof. God recognized this need in Gideon. He knew that in order for Gideon to overcome his fear, he needed proof so that he could go to the next level. And God answered Gideon twice with a supernatural intrusion into the laws of nature!

The care we need to take in using "fleeces" is that they may consist of varying circumstances that could just as easily take place without any input from God at all! We may say to ourselves, "If this light turns green before I reach the intersection . . . or if a certain song comes on the radio, God is speaking this or that to me." We really should accompany this kind of a fleece by scriptural confirmation and further guidance through prayer. One young man once told me that he was basing his decision about marrying a certain young woman on whether or not the next traffic light turned green or red. In my opinion, this was utter foolishness. Incidentally, the light turned red!

There are times when it is appropriate to ask for a sign—and God will answer. God responded to Gideon's lack of faith because He knew that Gideon's heart's desire was to obey. If the Lord knows that we want to obey, there are times when He will strengthen our faith by giving us a sign.

Seeking a sign is a valid way to ask God to speak to us in certain instances, but it should not be used exclusively for hearing from God. God does not always give us the solution to our dilemmas with instant answers, nor should we require Him to. God invites us to get to know Him and have a close relationship with Him so that we will recognize His voice in the many different ways in which He speaks.

Apply What You've Learned

I will place a wool fleece on the threshing floor. If there is dew only on the fleece and all the ground is dry, then I will know that you will save Israel by my hand, as you said.

JUDGES 6:37

1. For what reason might putting out a fleece not be the most preferred way to hear from God?

2. How can it be spiritually lazy to ask God for a sign?

3. Has God ever spoken to you through a sign? Explain.

22

Surprises

Anyone in a long-distance relationship knows that unexpectedly hearing a friend's voice over the telephone is a welcome surprise. Fresh communication is important for any relationship. God will sometimes astonish us through an unexpected revelation from Him. By now, it should not surprise us that God has many, many options to speak to us.

Sometimes God will speak through something we would never expect. For example, there is a story in the Bible of the Lord speaking through a donkey to Balaam the prophet (see Num. 22:21-34). At the time, Balaam was out of the will of God and trying to walk through a door the Lord had closed to him. So the Lord sent an angel to block Balaam and his donkey from continuing on. The donkey saw the angel, but Balaam did not . . . that is, until he beat the donkey to try to make it move, and the Lord caused the donkey to talk! Not only were Balaam's ears opened, but his eyes were opened as well. He saw an angel blocking their path with his sword drawn. God rebuked the greedy prophet in this quite unusual way to keep him from making a serious mistake.

One of the ways that God displays His sovereignty is by doing things we don't expect. We have a tendency to believe that God will work the same way we've seen Him work in the past. A study of the miraculous healings that Jesus performed during His earthly ministry shows that He almost never did it the same way twice. Sometimes He spoke. Sometimes He made mud using His own saliva. It was something different every time. Perhaps one of the ways we miss God most often is to ignore a message because it's coming in a form we simply did not expect.

God's Audible Voice

Although rare, God may even surprise us by speaking through an audible voice. God's people in both the Old and New Testaments on occasion heard His literal, audible words. We know about Adam, with whom God walked in the Garden of Eden. God also spoke audibly to the prophets, to the patriarchs and to Noah.

In the New Testament, people heard God's literal voice on a few occasions. Peter, James and John heard God's voice during the transfiguration. God spoke to Jesus at His baptism. The moment when Jesus came up out of the water, a voice from heaven said, "This is my Son, whom I love; with him I am well pleased" (Matt. 3:17).

One day, while Jesus was teaching, God spoke audibly (see John 12:29). Although the disciples heard God's audible voice and understood exactly what He spoke, some people heard God's voice as "thunder" and some thought an angel spoke. Apparently, most people did not hear discernible language but only a sound of some kind.

How could people hear the same voice and yet hear it differently? Could it be that it depended on the spiritual state of the person hearing? Not everyone was in a spiritual position to hear the voice as God's. Some probably thought it was just their imagination.

In Acts 9, at Paul's conversion on the Damascus road, Christ spoke directly to him, and those around him heard the same voice.

It is important for us not only to hear but also to hear with understanding. It is quite possible that to hear God's audible voice, we must be in a position to recognize it. Our hearts must be open to hear God, just as little Samuel's was when he finally realized the voice he was hearing was God's, and he responded in childlike faith, "Speak, Lord, I'm listening." In other words, it is easier to discern God's voice when we are in a close relationship with the Lord, like Samuel who was described in the Bible as one who "continually ministered before the Lord" (1 Sam. 3:1).

God Speaks Through a Non-Christian

It may surprise you, but God can also speak through unbelievers to get our attention. God spoke through a heathen king of Egypt to send a message to the godly King Josiah, telling him not to go to battle. King Josiah ignored this pagan's claim to be hearing from God; he went to war anyway and was killed (see 2 Chron. 35:20-24). God does not limit Himself only to using Christians or spiritually perfect messengers to communicate with us. When you think about it, if that were the case, He wouldn't use any of us as His messengers!

Probably the most likely way that God will speak to you through a non-Christian is through those who hold positions of authority in your life. For example, God can speak through your unbelieving boss or parent or teacher.

A Canadian Christian businessman told me recently that one of his most trusted advisors is another Canadian businessman who is not a believer. This man has been used greatly by the Lord to advise my friend in matters of business. The words he speaks to my friend are often the words of God for him.

Expect the Unexpected

I believe that God takes pleasure in surprises and the unexpected. A friend of ours was facing a time when she felt discouraged and stretched thin. Then God unexpectedly spoke to her through an unlikely source—a Barbie storybook. Late one night, she stopped at a grocery store to pick up some items to bake a treat for her elderly grandparents. She grumbled to herself as she stood waiting in line at the checkout. "Do I really need to take time for my elderly grandparents when I have so many other obligations?"

She absentmindedly picked up a children's storybook and began reading about how Barbie was scheduled to be in a competition but needed to help her elderly neighbor. Subsequently, she arrived late to the competition; however, the judges were so impressed with her that she won the prize anyway.

Our friend said, "I was convicted and encouraged to continue to serve my grandparents and trust God to take care of everything else in my life."

God loves surprises and wants us to grasp His purpose and message no matter how He delivers it. The Bible encourages us to trust Him to direct us: "Your ears will hear a word behind you, 'This is the way, walk in it,' whenever you turn to the right or to the left" (Isa. 30:21, *NASB*). He is faithful and will direct our path one step at a time. Let's tune our ears to hear His voice without preconceived ideas as to how He will speak.

Oswald Chambers said, "Jesus rarely comes where we expect Him; He appears where we least expect Him. . . . The only way a servant can remain true to God is to be ready for the Lord's surprise visits.

This readiness is expecting Jesus Christ at every turn. This sense of expectation will give our life the attitude of childlike wonder He wants it to have."[1]

Expect the unexpected. Call it what you will—a surprise, a suddenly, a "but God." Just know that at times, God may speak in surprising, dramatic and unpredictable ways!

Apply What You've Learned

VERSE TO REMEMBER:

Then the Lord opened the donkey's mouth.

NUMBERS 22:28

1. Why do you think God speaks to us in ways we would not expect?

2. Did God ever give you an unexpected revelation that you knew was His voice speaking personally to you?

3. Are you ready for God to surprise you?

Note

1. Oswald Chambers, *My Utmost for His Highest* (Grand Rapids, MI: Discovery House, 1992), March 29.

23

The Unique Way He Has Made Each of Us

It's a common desire for us to want other people's abilities and talents while taking our own for granted. People often describe their own talents with the phrase "I just . . ." or "I only . . ." Singers wish they could write books. Authors wish they could play the piano. Piano players wish they could paint portraits. Oftentimes people miss God's voice as He's trying to talk to them about their gifts while they are admiring someone else's.[1]

Your Unique Purpose

The Scriptures tell us to "train a child in the way he should go, and when he is old he will not turn from it" (Prov. 22:6). The "way he should go" in the Hebrew language means "according to his bent." God wires all of us differently. Individuals have different gifts or "bents" that allow them to hear from God according to the way He has made them.

We have each been given a purpose from God. If we are to define "purpose," we would say that it is the goal, the function, for which your life was conceived, the plan for which you were designed. A microphone, for example, "was born" with everything it needs to receive sounds and transmit them in the form of electrical impulses to an amplifier. It has inside of it each detail, each electronic component it needs to fulfill the task for which it "was born"—to receive sounds and transmit them.

If, instead of a microphone, I took a can opener and tried to use it to receive and transmit sounds, that can opener would be the most incompetent object ever imagined. The internal contents of the can opener enable it to fulfill the purpose for which it "was born," which does not include receiving and transmitting sounds. If I use the can opener to open cans, it will be a "fulfilled" object, because it "found" the purpose for which it exists.

God Speaks According to Your "Bent"

You were born containing all the components, all the traits, all the inclinations to fulfill your purpose in life. Everything you need is already inside of you. God "manufactured" you. He "knit you together." Your spiritual genetic code was designed by the Author of Life. Of course, you need to learn and be trained to use your gifts and talents.

When the prophet Jeremiah was born, he was already born with all the conditions, with all the heart and inclination, with the predisposition to be a prophet. If Jeremiah had been a musician, he would have been frustrated. If he had been a pastor, he would have been frustrated. If he had been an entrepreneur or a missionary, he would have been frustrated. He was born to be a prophet of God. At the moment that God called the prophet Jeremiah, he said, "Before I formed you in the womb I knew you, and before you were born I set you apart; I appointed you as a prophet to the nations" (Jer. 1:5).

Yes, God knew you even before you existed! It is hard to fathom, but the things of God are higher than what we understand; they are higher than our simplistic reasoning. Yet it gets even better. The most incredible part of the verse states that even before the birth of the prophet, he had already been appointed as such. Incredible! And because God has a purpose for each of us, and He has wired each of us differently, He often speaks to us according to the way we are wired.

God Speaks Through Your Motivational Gift

We have each been given different gifts at birth that express themselves in our different motivations.

> We have different gifts, according to the grace given us. If a man's gift is prophesying, let him use it in proportion to his faith. If it is serving, let him serve; if it is teaching, let him teach; if it is encouraging, let him encourage; if it is contributing to the needs of others, let him give generously; if it is leadership, let him govern diligently; if it is showing mercy, let him do it cheerfully (Rom. 12:3-8).

We each have different motivations in life, and the Lord often speaks to us through our personal motivation. For instance, if you have a motivational gift of giving, the Lord will probably speak to you about giving more than the average person, because you just love to give.

As a high school student, Sarah, who now oversees our church's publication department, began to realize that she had a talent for visual art. As her walk with God deepened, she recognized that God had given her these abilities and He probably wanted her to use the gifts she had been given. She began choosing classes that helped her develop those gifts. Sarah went on to study graphics design and loves her job as a graphics artist.

God wants us to enjoy what we are doing. If you cannot hold a tune, the Lord is not calling you to be a worship leader. That would waste your time as well as God's true call on your life, because He has not wired you for musical endeavors. Some people think that if the Lord speaks to them to do something, it will be something they hate doing. This could not be farther from the truth! God wired you perfectly to speak to you and fulfill His purpose through you.

Be Who God Made You to Be!

You should ask yourself, "What burns in the depths of my spirit? Am I hungry to learn more, to serve the Kingdom, to be a business owner, to be a pastor, a missionary, a prophet, an intercessor, an entrepreneur or used in the ministry of helping others?" A great evidence that shows that these thoughts are not mere daydreams of your mind is to ask, "Is my heart overflowing with joy and faith when I think about these things?" God has a purpose to be fulfilled in your life. He often answers that purpose through our natural gifts and abilities.

God-given gifts are the skills a person easily performs without formal training. For example, many songwriters just sit down and write the music they hear in their head. Some people are great at organizing, while others are natural counselors. We derive great pleasure from doing what we are naturally good at doing. God speaks to us through these natural gifts. Obviously, these natural gifts can be honed and developed with formal training.

If you aren't sure of your purpose in life, just do what you are good at doing, and then watch God corroborate your gift by blessing your endeavors. Do not spend your life trying to do what you are not gifted to do. I tried to minister to children in a Sunday School class but soon realized it was not my gift. When we started our new church, I preached one Sunday and ministered to the children in Sunday School the next. Those poor kids put up with me every other week! Teaching in the children's ministry was not what God had in mind for me to do.

I also had a tendency to get bogged down when I tried to be a counselor, because it was not how God has wired me. Yet I have traveled to dozens of nations, find myself ministering in a different city nearly every weekend and fly well over 100,000 miles each year. I have spent many nights sleeping on airplane seats because I need to immediately go to a meeting or radio station to speak when I land, and believe it or not, this energizes me. I come home from a long trip, having traveled to the other side of the world, and seldom experience jet lag. I have become comfortable with how God has made me and no longer try to be someone else. It has been so freeing.

How has the Lord wired you? Stop trying to be someone you are not.

Genesis 4:20-22 tells us that Jabal was the father of those who raised cattle. His brother Jubal was the father of all the musicians who played the lyre and pipe. His half-brother Tubal-Cain forged instruments made of bronze and iron. They all had different gifts from one another—specific gifts from the Lord.

God keeps our world in balance by giving each of us natural talents and pleasure in doing what needs to be done for the good of everyone around us. Aren't you glad everyone is not like you? All kinds of gifts and abilities are needed to get God's job done. God speaks to us and directs us through our natural talents and abilities.

When you get in touch with how God has wired you, the tasks that relate to that wiring will be a pleasure and not a burden. God will not violate your likes and dislikes. He will work in line with what you like to do. From the spiritual point of view, your heart leans toward and desires things that, since eternity, God has already brought into line for you to be involved in.

God has made you uniquely; you are one of a kind. He will speak to you and lead you according to the way He has shaped you for His service. Many times, when I have asked God what He wanted me to do in a specific situation, He has spoken to my heart, "Do what you want to do." He gives us more and more liberty as we grow spiritually into a state of maturity.

I often think of my own children. When they were young and inexperienced, my wife and I made all of their decisions for them; but as they grew older and more mature, we let them do more of what they wanted to do according to how the Lord made them.

Maybe you are trying to hear from God about your life, when in actuality He is speaking to you already through the way He has made you. Trust those inner leadings and nudges that come from the way God has wired you.

Apply What You've Learned

VERSE TO REMEMBER:

Train a child in the way he should go [according to his bent], and when he is old he will not turn from it.

PROVERBS 22:6

1. What are your particular strengths and preferences that cause you to hear God most often in a certain way?

2. How do you nurture the natural gifts that God has given you?

3. What burns in the depths of your spirit? Does God speak to you through this desire?

Note

1. Many thanks to my friend Marcelo Almeida from Sao Paulo, Brazil, for insights included in this chapter.

24

History

God is not haphazard or random. There is always continuity and unity in His plan of dealing with mankind down through the ages. He speaks to us through history and wants us to learn from past mistakes. In the New Testament, Paul warned the early Christians not to fall into the same sin as the murmuring and rebellious Israelites in the Old Testament.

Now these things occurred as examples to keep us from setting our hearts on evil things as they did (1 Cor. 10:6).

When the Israelites complained because of their monotonous meals of manna, and they believed that the promises of God had failed, they were punished because they refused to trust in and obey God. History was repeating itself in the Early Church. The New Testament Christians were tempted to participate in the feasts celebrated in the pagan temples, and the apostle Paul warned them not to expose themselves to this immorality and disobey God like the Israelites had. He was, in essence, encouraging them to hear God through history and not make the same mistakes their forebears had.

History Repeats for a Reason

God has spoken to me so often by what He has done in history. If God does something in the past, He does so for a reason—to teach us a lesson for the future. For example, take the prophet Elijah. We usually think of Elijah as a super prophet who heard God and had a direct line of communication with Him. Elijah had to be extraordinary, didn't he, if he got translated into heaven without dying? Yet James (see James 5) seems to be making the point that Elijah was not superhuman, but was a mere man. He was subject to the same weaknesses that you and I have. He was liable to the same limitations.

Elijah was a man just like us. He prayed earnestly that it would not rain, and it did not rain on the land for three and a half years. Again he prayed, and the heavens gave rain, and the earth produced its crops (Jas. 5:17-19).

God worked a miracle in answer to Elijah's prayer; and since Elijah is "just like us," it is reasonable to presume that God will also hear our prayers in the same way He heard and blessed Elijah.

Praying for History to Repeat Itself

In the early 1900s, a series of mighty spiritual revivals began in Wales that spread throughout central Europe, Norway and Scandinavia, and even to Africa, India, China and Korea. Not too long ago, I joined thousands of Korean youth in a stadium in Seoul, Korea. We were praying all night for another visitation of the Lord's Spirit like the Welsh revival of 100 years ago that spread to Korea. We were praying for history to repeat itself and for God to bring another awakening to this great nation.

I often share with thousands of God's people all over the world that I pray for God to visit His people in our generation, both young and old together, in such a way that we will experience His power and presence like never before in our families, our churches, our communities and our nations. Acts 2:17-18 declares boldly and clearly:

"In the last days," God says, "I *will* pour out my Spirit on all people. Your sons and daughters *will* prophesy, your young men *will* see visions, your old men *will* dream dreams. Even on my servants, both men and women, I *will* pour out my Spirit in those days, and they *will* prophesy" (emphasis added).

This Scripture was fulfilled at Pentecost—yet God desires an even greater fulfillment as thousands more turn to Him and receive the outpouring of His Holy Spirit. He is simply asking us to pray. Remember the words of John Wesley: "God does everything by prayer and nothing without it."

God is a speaking God, down through the ages. From Genesis through Revelation God has spoken to His people. If we listen for His voice throughout biblical history, we can hear Him speak to us today. Even though He never changes, He reveals Himself to us in ways that we can understand today.

Nothing New Under the Sun

The Scriptures tell us "there is no new thing under the sun." Ecclesiastes says it like this: "What has been will be again, what has been done will be done again; there is nothing new under the sun. Is there anything of which one can say, 'Look! This is something new'? It was here already, long ago; it was here before our time" (Eccles. 1:9-10).

Many times I have thought that I was facing a problem or difficulty no one else had ever faced, only to find out by reading a history book that people in generations before me faced the same dilemma. By reading their stories, I discovered how people just like me overcame their problems, and the Lord used it to speak to me to find answers to my own problems.

When I served as a senior pastor for 15 years, many times I had to lead people through change. Sometimes this was very difficult. One day, I read the following story from history, and the Lord used it to grant me patience with those who were slow to change. This is a letter written by Martin Van Buren, then governor of New York, to President Jackson, concerning what he considered an "evil" new business enterprise threatening the United States:

January 31, 1829

To President Jackson,
The canal system of this country is being threatened by the spread of a new form of transportation known as "railroads." The federal government must preserve the canals for the following reasons:

1. If canal boats are supplanted by "railroads," serious unemployment will result. Captains, cooks, drivers, hostlers, repairmen and lock tenders will be left without means of livelihood, not to mention the numerous farmers now employed in growing hay for the horses.

2. Boat builders would suffer, and towline, whip and harness makers would be left destitute.

3. Canal boats are absolutely essential to defend the United States. In the event of the expected trouble with England,

the Erie Canal would be the only means by which we could move the supplies so vital to waging modern war.

As you may well know, Mr. President, "railroad" carriages are pulled at the enormous speed of fifteen miles per hour by "engines" which, in addition to endangering life and limb of passengers, roar and snort their way through the country-side, setting fire to crops, scaring the livestock and frightening women and children. The Almighty certainly never intended that people should travel at such breakneck speed.

Martin Van Buren, Governor of New York[1]

Our twenty-first-century minds can have a good chuckle at this future president of the United States who was extremely resistant to a change that was inevitable. (Nothing could stop the coming of the railroad!) But the Lord used this story from history to speak to me about how hard change is for most people. As a shepherd who was leading God's people, I realized that God was asking me to be patient with those who were struggling with change.

If we are going to grow and mature, we must be ready to embrace change. And when the Lord has "change" in store, we can trust that He knows best and that He has a great future on our horizon.

Apply What You've Learned

VERSE TO REMEMBER:

Now these things occurred as examples.
1 CORINTHIANS 10:6

1. How does knowledge of how God spoke in the past help us hear from Him today?
2. How exactly do we learn from past mistakes?
3. Why is change so difficult for us?

Note

1. Martin Van Buren, cited in "Dynamic Preaching," *Net Results Magazine*, March 1991, p. 30.

25

Different Cultures

My friend Mark and his family spent a month living in Central Asia, assisting missionaries in a country where Christianity was not officially tolerated. It was an excellent opportunity to be immersed in the culture and experience everyday life there. One of their favorite memories was of buying fresh bread every morning. It was a flat bread baked in a clay oven and served piping hot.

They soon came to realize how important bread is to that society. At the beginning of every meal, the host took the bread from the center of the table, broke it and set out pieces for everyone to share. Right there in the midst of their culture was a picture of Jesus, the Bread of Life whose body was broken for all to partake. Whether we realize it or not, God is speaking in and through different cultures, because He wants to draw all men to Himself.

Every culture has a redemptive purpose from God's perspective. God speaks to every culture in its own specific heart language. Paul heard Jesus speak to him in Hebrew, his native tongue, his heart language. You hear God speak to you in your native language. Missionaries spend months learning the language of the people they serve so that they can communicate in that people's heart language. But it must be more than syntax and vocabulary. The heart language of a person must take into account a person's whole culture. God speaks to a person through his culture.

Paul points out that God made all the cultures that are scattered in diverse nations—He created culture, race, ethnicity—and He knows exactly what each person will respond to.

> From one man he made every nation of men, that they should inhabit the whole earth; and he determined the times set for them and the exact places where they should live (Acts 17:25-27).

Knowing and understanding a culture helps us understand how God is speaking in light of that culture. Throughout the Old Testament,

God chose to reveal Himself to mankind through the Hebrew culture. To understand what He is saying to us today, it seems important that we learn to interpret the Bible within its historical and cultural context.

In Acts 2:9-12, the disciples declared the wonders of God in the many languages of those who were visiting Jerusalem for the feast of Pentecost. These peoples from different cultures and languages, scattered throughout the Mediterranean world, were amazed that simple Galileans knew their languages. Because God spoke so uniquely within their culture, they received the good news in their diverse native languages and joined in praise to God while experiencing His miraculous presence and acts.

Paul, the apostle, loved people and wanted to win them to Christ. But God had called him to a people vastly different from his own. Paul was an educated Israelite whose thinking and values were shaped by Jewish religious law. Yet God called him to the Gentiles, a people who knew nothing about Jewish law. Paul knew that if he learned to think like the Gentiles, whose way of thinking was radically different from his own, he could know what God was saying to them and how to reach them in the Lord's name.

> Though I am free and belong to no man, I make myself a slave to everyone, to win as many as possible. To the Jews I became like a Jew, to win the Jews. To those under the law I became like one under the law (though I myself am not under the law), so as to win those under the law. To those not having the law I became like one not having the law (though I am not free from God's law but am under Christ's law), so as to win those not having the law. To the weak I became weak, to win the weak. I have become all things to all men so that by all possible means I might save some. I do all this for the sake of the gospel, that I may share in its blessings (1 Cor. 9:19-23).

Different cultures not only speak different languages, but their thought processes and thought patterns are also different. Paul said that he learned how different people thought so that he could speak their language using thoughts and words they would understand. That's how God also speaks—in a way that is understandable to each particular culture.

Individual Christians hear God in the context of their own culture, but they also have the responsibility to think and see through the mind and eye of other cultures if they want to make Jesus understandable to them.

During a visit to a village near Darfur, in Sudan, my friend Ibrahim had an unexpected but divine appointment with an Islamic sultan, the leader of the region. These peoples were reconsidering their relationship with the Arabs and with Islam as a religion and mentioned they wanted a religion that respected their culture and did not look down on their dark skin.

When Ibrahim learned that the sultan was sick and using medication, he respectfully asked the sultan if he could pray for him and use the name of Jesus in prayer. The sultan was in agreement. Ibrahim then prayed for the sultan's healing.

The next morning, as they were getting ready to board a helicopter, Ibrahim heard someone shouting his name: "Ibrahim, Ibrahim!" He turned and saw the sultan on horseback, galloping toward him. Ibrahim ran back just as the sultan jumped off the horse. He gave Ibrahim a big hug and then started stretching his legs and arms while shouting, "I am healed, I am healed!"

Ibrahim was respectful of the sultan and his culture and seized the opportunity to pray a specific and compassionate prayer ordered by God. God moved and met the sultan at his point of need. God desires to bring all people to Himself, and He will do it within the context of a person's culture.

In order to communicate with cultures different from our own, we have to learn to communicate with understanding and compassion and know the vocabulary and thought processes. Frequently there are entire countries and cultures that are kept in darkness by lies from the enemy. These strongholds become cornerstones of a particular culture, according to John Dawson, in his book *Taking Our Cities for God*:

> Take, for example, the struggle with rejection and fear of authority experienced by many Australians, because their country originated as a penal colony. Entering through these cruel roots of Australian history, Satan has been able to create a general distrust of all authority figures, including the highest of all who is, of course, God Himself. The truth is

that Australia is not a nation founded on rejection and injustice, but a chosen people with as much dignity and potential as any people in history. They are a people greatly loved by a heavenly Father who is calling them to healing and purpose.

Even individual cities have strongholds that keep God from moving until they are recognized. Your city is God's city. The people are made in His image. Satan is an invader and usurper operating in our territory. . . . An obvious example would be the spirit of greed which was let loose during the California gold rush and still dominates the culture of Los Angeles and San Francisco to this day.[1]

Praying Christians realize that God has a redemptive purpose for every city and culture, and they can make a difference by praying specifically for God to pour out revelation concerning His redemptive plans for that city or culture.

God has often used various cultures to speak to me of His love, compassion and grace. I learned years ago from watching people sweeping the streets at 5:30 A.M. in Seoul, Korea, how our God values work. Hard work has been a part of Korean culture for generations. I have learned from many of my Latin American friends the importance of relationships and family. My African friends have taught me unselfish love and generosity when they invite me into their homes for a meal. My friends in India have modeled for me a deep respect and honor for their parents. God uses each culture to speak to us about Himself and His attributes. Different cultures teach us how much we need one another and can learn from each other.

Although God speaks through various cultures, there are also things in most cultures that are not honoring to God. In these cases, Kingdom culture always supersedes local culture.

I have felt embarrassed when I've heard the words and actions of foreigners in other nations that were filled with pride and arrogance, thereby dishonoring the Lord's redemptive purpose in that foreign culture. God has so much to teach us, but arrogance can blind our eyes from hearing His voice clearly.

Every culture has a redemptive purpose from God that needs to be honored. Our God speaks to us by using these cultures to model His purposes.

Apply What You've Learned

VERSE TO REMEMBER:

*I have become all things to all men so that by all possible means
I might save some. I do all this for the sake of the gospel,
that I may share in its blessings.*
1 CORINTHIANS 9:22

1. How does knowledge of a culture help us understand how God speaks to others?

2. How do strongholds in a culture hinder people from hearing Him?

3. Give an example of how God speaks to you through your own culture.

Note
1. John Dawson, *Taking Our Cities for God* (Lake Mary, FL: Creation House, 1989), pp. 79-80.

26

People's Lives

"Your life is the only Bible some people will ever read" is an axiom that often rings true. People are watching how Christians live. They can see whether or not a Christian's lifestyle corresponds with what he or she says. If a believer's words and actions are not consistent, a non-Christian's view of God may be skewed. How we live is a direct reflection of how we represent Jesus Christ!

Sometimes God speaks so clearly through someone that we just know that He is speaking to us. Sue, a pastor's wife, tells of the time her sister-in-law, Cheryl, was battling cancer and was very frail and weak. A few women, including Sue's 80-year-old mother, gathered for a time of worship and prayer. After praying fervently for Cheryl, who couldn't talk at this time due to the swelling of her tongue, they offered prayer for Sue's 80-year-old mother as well. Cheryl wanted to stand up to pray, but she was too weak. Sue's mother offered her lap so that Cheryl would not have to stand.

What Sue observed next was Jesus, the one who gives comfort, in action as Cheryl curled up on Sue's mother's lap like an infant. Usually Sue's mother was reserved, but she held Cheryl like a baby, and they wept together. Sue recalls, "The picture was one of those impressionable moments when you see God working through one person to another to minister love, healing and comfort. It was, without a doubt, Jesus showing up and saying, 'I am here, and I love you.'"

God Speaks Through Imperfect People

God has designed His work to be accomplished perfectly—through imperfect people. We are often tempted to think, *How could God ever use me? I don't know how to help anyone else. I'm afraid. I don't know the Bible well enough. I need to get my life more together.* If you feel this way, you have a lot of company.

Moses complained to the Lord that he could not speak properly. Jeremiah informed the Lord that he was too young. Joshua was scared, and the Lord kept reassuring him to be of good courage and that He would be with Joshua just as He was with Moses. Gideon thought he was brought up in the wrong family for the Lord to use him. The list could go on and on.

Even Paul, the apostle, admitted to the Corinthian church that he had a deep sense of his own weaknesses that caused him to feel fearful and inadequate: "When I came to you, brothers, I did not come with eloquence or superior wisdom as I proclaimed to you the testimony about God. . . . I came to you in weakness and fear, and with much trembling" (1 Cor. 2:1,3).

Nevertheless, Paul goes on to declare that although his speech was not persuasive, the Holy Spirit's power was in his words. Second Timothy 1:7 says it another way: "For God did not give us a spirit of timidity, but a spirit of power, of love and of self-discipline." Insecurities can keep us paralyzed so that we never move beyond our comfort zone. However, if we trust God, as have those who have gone on before us, He will allow us to use our gifts and even increase them to help others. He will give us courage and resolution. God's love will always win over the fear of man.

Sometimes the Lord brings a brother or sister who is like "sandpaper" in our life. Something about this person rubs us the wrong way. Could it be that God is putting us to the test to hear His voice through this abrasive person? If we do not learn the lesson from relating to the person, the Lord will probably bring someone else who may be even tougher to handle. Welcome to the real world!

God Speaks Through Observation

I am a people watcher. I remember when, as a young pastor, I was in Ohio at a leadership meeting and was able to observe a well-known servant of the Lord behind the scenes. He was the kind of person who took every opportunity to notice those around him and was sensitive to their needs. As I watched one day, this man of God led a busboy to the Lord. Then he went out of his way to help this young man find a local church to attend the following weekend. I found this particular leader serving wherever he found an opportunity. His life had a profound impact on me. He was a true leader—one I wanted to model my life after. His life spoke volumes to others, and God spoke to me through his life.

In John 13, we read that Jesus sent His disciples to prepare the Passover. When Jesus arrived, He realized there was a problem. The disciples were arguing about who should wash their feet. Since there was no servant present, and it was customary for a servant to wash the feet of the family and guests as they came in from the dusty streets, the disciples were frustrated.

Without a word, Jesus took a towel and wrapped it around Himself. He knelt down and began to wash the disciples' feet. The disciples learned by observing Jesus without a word being spoken.

Your "Witness"

Often people come to a personal relationship with Jesus Christ because they see God working through someone's life. A friend of mine shared his faith in Christ with a salesman who came into his place of business. The salesman noticed that my friend had a sense of peace in his life even though he was going through many problems with family and business. Later the salesman received the Lord and got involved with believers in a small group in his local area. The small group began to pray for the salesman's unsaved mother. She received the Lord a few weeks before she passed away.

The Bible says that we are witnesses. An eyewitness has seen something, and he or she becomes a vessel to speak of what has been witnessed. How does the world hear about God's salvation? By hearing the testimony of God's people, who have the mark of God on them. Like the disciples who testified about what they had learned and seen while they were with Jesus, we, as God's people, help others understand God's love when they see it demonstrated through us. God's promises in His Word are confirmed in the lives of His people. Others will hear God speak through our lives because we are His witnesses. We are salt in our society, lights set on a hill, representatives of His kingdom.

Billy Graham is one of my heroes. He is probably one of the most well-known Christian leaders of our generation and has been a close confidant of many presidents and prime ministers. And yet he has maintained a life-long walk of deep humility. He has finished well. In a generation when so many Christian leaders have fallen due to pride, lust and the love of money, the Lord has used Billy Graham as a model to speak to me and countless others.

Paul, the apostle, was not afraid to say that he was a role model: "Follow my example, as I follow the example of Christ" (1 Cor. 11:1). Since Christ was his model in all things, Paul knew that if others followed him as he followed Christ, they would not go astray. Let's live as Jesus-followers for others to see and thus allow God to speak to them.

Apply What You've Learned

VERSE TO REMEMBER:

Follow my example, as I follow the example of Christ.
1 CORINTHIANS 11:1

1. How are you a role model to help someone hear from God?

2. Have you ever experienced God speaking to you as you observed someone's life?

3. What would your life look like if you lived as a light on a hill or as salt in society? (Think of some practical ways that you could make a difference for Christ in your sphere of influence.)

27

Stories and Parables

While going through a very difficult time with her sick husband, Sharon would often work outside in her flower beds just to have time alone. However, she soon learned that she wasn't alone; the Lord was right there beside her. Just as Jesus taught in parables when He walked this earth, He now began to talk to Sharon about what she was doing in the garden and then proceeded with a spiritual application. Sharon began to dig into His Word to find all those principles from the garden so that she could understand more about what God was teaching her and apply it to her circumstances.

When Jesus lived on Earth, He taught using the common heart language of the people. He spoke in stories, parables and proverbs, which were word pictures the common people understood. As a result, those who heard were able to understand and apply the spiritual truths Jesus taught, and their lives were transformed.

> Jesus spoke all these things to the crowd in parables; he did not say anything to them without using a parable. So was fulfilled what was spoken through the prophet: "I will open my mouth in parables, I will utter things hidden since the creation of the world" (Matt. 13:34-36).

Jesus knew that spiritual things are often not tangible until we "see" a natural illustration that points us to the spiritual parallel. God is a great storyteller! He told stories of a sower sowing seeds, a lost sheep, a hidden treasure and more to help the people understand what He was saying about God and His kingdom.

Jesus' stories—His parables—often had double meanings. There was first the literal meaning, apparent to anyone; but there was also a deeper meaning about God's truth and His kingdom. For example, the parable of the leaven (see Matt. 13:33) describes how yeast transforms dough into bread. A deeper meaning is that we are transformed when we allow God's Word to take root in our hearts. And we are the leaven that transforms the society in which we live and work.

Spiritual truths are spiritually discerned. Jesus also told His disciples that some would not understand His parables. "To you it has been given to know the secrets of the kingdom of God; but for others they are in parables, so that seeing they may not see, and hearing they may not hear" (Luke 8:10). Jesus was aware that some people who heard His parables would not understand because their hearts were closed to what the Spirit of God was saying. They had unbelief in their hearts. God can only reveal the secrets of His kingdom to the person who acknowledges his or her need for God.

When God spoke to David through the prophet Nathan about his sin, He used a story.

> There were two men in a certain town, one rich and the other poor. The rich man had a very large number of sheep and cattle, but the poor man had nothing except one little ewe lamb he had bought. He raised it, and it grew up with him and his children. It shared his food, drank from his cup and even slept in his arms. It was like a daughter to him. Now a traveler came to the rich man, but the rich man refrained from taking one of his own sheep or cattle to prepare a meal for the traveler who had come to him. Instead, he took the ewe lamb that belonged to the poor man and prepared it for the one who had come to him.
>
> When David heard this story, he burned with anger against the man and said to Nathan, "As surely as the Lord lives, the man who did this deserves to die! He must pay for that lamb four times over, because he did such a thing and had no pity."
>
> Then Nathan said to David, "You are the man!" (2 Sam. 12:1-7).

God used Nathan to help David see his own sin.

In the New Testament, we see the story of an expert in the law who stood up to test Jesus. He asked Jesus what he must do to inherit eternal life. In turn, Jesus asked him what the Scriptures said. The man answered:

> "Love the Lord your God with all your heart and with all your soul and with all your strength and with all your mind; and, love your neighbor as yourself."
>
> "You have answered correctly," Jesus replied. "Do this and you will live."

But the expert wanted to justify himself, so he asked Jesus, "And who is my neighbor?" (Luke 10:27-29).

In reply, Jesus told a story about a man who was going down from Jerusalem to Jericho. When he fell into the hands of robbers, he was rescued by a Samaritan who had mercy on him after two religious leaders just walked by without offering help. Then Jesus asked, "Which of these three do you think was a neighbor to the man who fell into the hands of robbers?" The expert in the law replied, "The one who had mercy on him." Jesus told him, "Go and do likewise" (Luke 10:36-37).

Certainly Jesus could have simply told the religious leader to be a man of mercy, but He chose to use a parable to drive home the real meaning of this truth. Sometimes we call a parable an earthly story with a heavenly meaning.

During the past few months, I have been teaching a group of new Christians stories from the Old Testament. I love to see the excitement on their faces when I tell the stories of Joseph and his coat of many colors, Noah and the ark, Jonah and the whale and Daniel in the lion's den. These stories have great spiritual insights and wisdom for our generation as they teach us to obey the living God. God speaks to us again and again through stories and parables.

Speaking of stories, your own testimony is probably the most powerful story you have. We will see how the Lord speaks through our testimonies in chapter 32.

Apply What You've Learned

VERSE TO REMEMBER:

Jesus spoke all these things to the crowd in parables; he did not say anything to them without using a parable.
MATTHEW 13:34

1. How are God's messages to us more tangible when we see a natural illustration?

2. Describe how a parable or story helped you understand God's voice.

3. How can a story or parable change your life?

Section Five

WISDOM, COUNSEL AND THE CHURCH

28

Commonsense Wisdom

The first time you go hiking and camping in the snow, you are told that certain things you do out in the wilderness are simply common sense. You may not be sure what this means the first time you go winter camping, but you soon realize that keeping your socks dry is common sense. After one experience of wet socks and the consequences of frozen socks, the next time your experience will tell you that it is just common sense to keep your feet dry!

It is amazing to me that so many people seem to think that common sense must vanish in order for them to be really spiritual. It is often just the opposite. God has gifted us with common sense.

Common sense is an ability to look at things in a straightforward way. It is mostly based on our experiences and not on our knowledge. In other words, our previous experiences add up to knowing intuitively what makes sense in a certain situation. As we accumulate more wisdom throughout life, we can automatically sense what to do in a given situation because it is based on our past experiences. We can use our own sound judgment to make a decision.

Wisdom goes hand in hand with common sense. I like to call it "commonsense wisdom." Straight thinking is the result of both experience and wisdom. The Bible emphasizes that we should ask for wisdom. "If any of you lacks wisdom, he should ask God, who gives generously to all without finding fault, and it will be given to him" (Jas. 1:5). Our God desires to give us wisdom. If we only ask and believe, He will give it to us.

The book of Proverbs is a great source for commonsense wisdom. I encourage you to read at least a few verses of Proverbs or Psalms on a regular basis. The book of Psalms encourages us, builds us up and helps us express our innermost feelings. The book of Proverbs, with its commonsense wisdom, shows us how to stay out of trouble.

Read through the following Scriptures on commonsense wisdom from the books of Psalms and Proverbs, and take your time as you read.

The man who knows right from wrong and has good judgment and common sense is happier than the man who is immensely rich! For such wisdom is far more valuable than precious jewels. Nothing else compares with it (Prov. 3:13, *TLB*).

Have two goals: wisdom—that is, knowing and doing right—and common sense. Don't let them slip away, for they fill you with living energy and bring you honor and respect (Prov. 3:21-22, *TLB*).

"Learn to be wise," he said, "and develop good judgment and common sense! I cannot overemphasize this point" (Prov. 4:5, *TLB*).

Getting wisdom is the most important thing you can do! And with your wisdom, develop common sense and good judgment (Prov. 4:7, *TLB*).

Men with common sense are admired as counselors (Prov. 10:13, *TLB*).

A godly man gives good advice, but a rebel is destroyed by lack of common sense (Prov. 10:21, *TLB*).

A mocker never finds the wisdom he claims he is looking for, yet it comes easily to the man with common sense (Prov. 14:6, *TLB*).

Wisdom is enshrined in the hearts of men of common sense (Prov. 14:33, *TLB*).

The wise man is known by his common sense (Prov. 16:21, *TLB*).

For I am your servant; therefore give me common sense to apply your rules to everything I do (Ps. 119:124-125, *TLB*).

If you want favor with both God and man, and a reputation for good judgment and common sense, then trust the Lord completely; don't ever trust yourself (Prov. 3:3-4, *TLB*).

Any enterprise is built by wise planning, becomes strong through common sense, and profits wonderfully by keeping abreast of the facts (Prov. 24:3, *TLB*).

Our God-given common sense has a remarkable capacity to interpret our current situation in light of our history and God's Word. As we hear God speak to us, we can then make a godly decision rather than a foolish one.

Exercising Common Sense

Paul, the apostle, told the Corinthian Christians that they should learn to judge small matters among themselves, because at the end of this age, the resurrected saints will help judge the world and even angels (see 1 Cor. 6:2-3). As Christians, we can learn to exercise good and wise judgment (common sense) right now, in this life.

When we walk in the Spirit, we are in tune with God's voice and can make commonsense decisions according to God's will and wisdom.

In Acts, the Jerusalem church leaders made a decision by saying, "It seemed good to the Holy Spirit and to us" (Acts 15:28). God entrusts us, as His children, to use our common sense as we seek the Spirit's guidance.

Common sense will guide you when it comes to making monetary decisions. You will not go into debt when you do not spend more money than you earn. The Holy Spirit does not need to speak in an audible voice to tell us that we cannot have more money going out than we have coming in.

For the sake of example, let's say that I am wondering if the Lord wants me to buy a new car. If I don't sense anything from God, then one of the commonsense things I must ask myself is, "Can I afford it?" If I can't afford it, commonsense wisdom tells me not to buy it. The audible voice of God or a prophecy or a dream or a vision is not needed when commonsense wisdom is already telling me what to do.

When Common Sense Clashes with Peace

Not everything that seems like common sense will be the voice of God speaking. I grew up as an only son. My father trained me to operate the family farm with the eventual goal of owning it. In the late 1970s, when the Lord began to call me toward full-time ministry, I just did not have God's peace about staying on the farm. Although it seemed like common sense to stay in a career I had been trained for, it clashed with my peace of mind. I knew the Lord was speaking to me about giving up the opportunity to own the farm and instead giving myself to serve as a pastor of a local church, which I did for the next 15 years.

When God's Voice Seems at Odds with Common Sense

There are times when God speaks and it will go against what you think is common sense. I am sure the widow in 1 Kings 17 had second thoughts about giving her last flour and oil to Elijah. It just did not make sense to make a meal for Elijah when she and her son were about to starve. But Elijah told the widow that God had spoken, and the flour and oil would not run dry. Their obedience to the Lord's voice caused a supernatural miracle of abundance.

God's voice seemed to be the opposite of common sense in another biblical story in 2 Kings 5. The prophet Elisha told Naaman to dip himself in the Jordan River seven times and he would be healed of leprosy. Common sense might tell you that washing yourself in a dirty river would not be good for your health. Additionally, common sense would tell you that if you dipped in one time and were not cured, six more times wouldn't bring the healing either. But Naaman chose to trust that God was speaking through the prophet even though it did not make sense. He dipped himself seven times and then was healed.

God Encourages Commonsense Decisions

I have found that if God doesn't speak to me specifically, it doesn't mean He is not leading me. There are some issues about which God already trusts me. Many times, you know what is right or wrong and you know the way in which to go. You don't need a specific "word" from God; however, you must always stay open to waiting on Him to see if He needs to intervene in your plans.

God tells us to do the seeking and He will speak. We can be assured that He *is* the Spirit of wisdom and He will not lead us to do things or make decisions that are unwise.

Apply What You've Learned

VERSE TO REMEMBER:

The wise man is known by his common sense.
PROVERBS 16:21, *TLB*

1. How do wisdom and common sense go hand in hand?

2. Have you ever been in a situation when something that seemed like common sense was not God speaking? What did you do?

3. Did God's voice ever seem the opposite of common sense? What did you do?

29

The Local Church

Every Christian needs the close support of a church family to help him or her hear from God. The Bible says, "But encourage one another daily, as long as it is called Today, so that none of you may be hardened by sin's deceitfulness" (Heb. 3:13). It is extremely difficult to live the Christian life alone. Believers need fellowship and encouragement from one another daily.

The Church is not a building or a meeting or a program. The church of Jesus Christ is simply *people*. As believers, we are the Church. The word "church" literally means "called-out ones." The Church, then, is a group of people who have been called out of spiritual darkness into the light of God's kingdom.

The Universal Body of Christ

When we come to Christ, we are immediately a part of the greater Body of Christ, or the universal Church, which includes every believer who has ever named the name of Christ from every nation of the world. Jesus talks about His universal Church in the gospels. "And I tell you that you are Peter, and on this rock I will build my church, and the gates of Hades will not overcome it" (Matt. 16:18).

I have had the privilege of traveling to six continents of the world. Everywhere I go I find believers from completely different backgrounds, with different skin colors and different cultures, but with one thing in common: They all have received Jesus Christ as Lord and are part of the same family. They are the Body of Christ worldwide. Paul, the apostle, recognized this global Church when he said, "For this reason I kneel before the Father, from whom his whole family in heaven and on earth derives its name" (Eph. 3:14-15).

The Local Body of Christ

The word "church" also refers to the *local* Church—the local Body of Christ. Within God's universal Church family are *local* churches in each community that provide the support and love each believer needs. Whether you are a part of a local community church, a megachurch or a small house church, the Lord wants to speak to you through the leadership there and through fellow believers.

Every believer needs a "support system" in order to survive. We get that support system from being committed to other believers in a local church and having regular fellowship with them. We are a part of a spiritual family—a family of the redeemed. This spiritual family gives us a place to grow and learn from other believers how to live the Christian life. We need this input from others.

Sometimes, through disillusionment, disappointment or spiritual pride, believers find themselves uninvolved in a local church. This leaves them very vulnerable. The Bible tells us that "no temptation has seized you except what is common to man. And God is faithful; he will not let you be tempted beyond what you can bear. But when you are tempted, he will also provide a way out so that you can stand up under it" (1 Cor. 10:13).

The local church is often "the way out" that the Lord has prepared for His people to withstand the onslaught of Satan's attacks. When we fellowship with other believers, we realize that we are not alone in the temptations we face. We receive spiritual protection, strength and oversight from the spiritual leaders the Lord has placed in our life, and God speaks to us through them. The Lord's plan is to use the local church to protect us, help us grow and equip us to be all that we can be in Jesus Christ.

D. L. Moody, an evangelist from the late 1800s, was used of the Lord to lead a million people to Christ. Many times when he preached, he had a choir that included singers from many churches in the community in which he was preaching. A lady came to him one day and said, "Mr. Moody, I would like to sing in your choir." When Moody asked her which local church she represented, she said, "I am involved in the universal church."

Moody said to her, "Then find the pastor of the universal church and sing in his choir." In other words, Moody was concerned about this lady's lack of involvement in a local church. He recognized the need to be committed to a local church for spiritual protection and accountability. Though the church is not perfect, God designed the church to be a blessing to believers. The church might have some spots and wrinkles, but she is still engaged to the Bridegroom, and He is committed to make her beautiful.

Brett Monk, a pastor friend from the Washington, DC, area, believes it is difficult to hear from God without being a part of a local church. I believe his assessment is correct.

> It has become really popular to say that you love God but don't like the church or "organized religion." The church is the bride of Christ. How many husbands would want to be friends with someone who said they like you but don't like your wife? Many people have been hurt by church leaders or by church people. I know I have. That doesn't excuse us from being connected with God's people. I've eaten food that's made me sick, but I haven't given up on food. I've gotten injured while playing sports I enjoy, but that doesn't stop me from playing. I've been in car accidents, but I still drive. I'm not sure how you could ever expect to accurately hear from God without being part of a local church.

God's Mouthpiece

Spiritual leaders as well as other believers in the local church are there to exhort us, comfort us and uphold us in prayer. God places spiritual leaders in our life who are accountable to God and also to other spiritual leaders to watch out for us.

> Remember your leaders, who spoke the Word of God to you. Consider the outcome of their way of life and imitate their faith. Obey your leaders and submit to their authority. They keep watch over you as men who must give an account. Obey them so that their work will be a joy, not a burden, for that would be of no advantage to you (Heb. 13:7,17).

Spiritual leaders give us spiritual protection, and we need to follow their example as they place their faith in Jesus Christ. We should remember them, receive the Word of God from them, obey them, be submissive to them and do all that we can to make their responsibility joyful and not a burden. God often uses them as His mouthpiece to speak to us. The Bible tells us that the devil is like a roaring lion seeking to devour us. Lions prey on strays, those who are isolated from the herd. That's why we need our spiritual family, the local church, and our church leaders, to protect us and encourage us. The Lord has called us to recognize and honor them.

> Now we ask you, brothers, to respect those who work hard among you, who are over you in the Lord and who admonish you. Hold them in the highest regard in love because of their work. Live in peace with each other (1 Thess. 5:12-13).

I have spent much time traveling to various nations of the world in the past years, and I have been blessed over and over again by the spiritual leaders the Lord has placed in my life. Our small-group leaders, local pastors and elders have provided a tremendous sense of encouragement and protection to me and to my family.

Many times these precious brothers and sisters in Christ have prayed, encouraged and exhorted us, and the Lord has used them to hold me accountable to take enough time with my family even though my travel schedule can be demanding. I am grateful to the Lord for using spiritual leaders in my life to speak to me again and again, because I know that I need them in my life.

Because you cannot accomplish all that you want to on your own, God will be faithful to speak to you through the spiritual leaders and fellow believers He has placed in your life within your local church.

Apply What You've Learned

VERSE TO REMEMBER:

Obey your leaders and submit to their authority. They keep watch over you as men who must give an account. Obey them so that their work will be a joy, not a burden, for that would be of no advantage to you.
HEBREWS 13:17

1. Why is a community of believers so important to your hearing from God?

2. Explain how you receive a support system from the local church.

3. How has God used others in your church as His mouthpiece to speak to you?

30

The Whole Body of Christ

We've just learned how the Lord uses those who preach the word in our local churches to speak to us, but the Lord also uses preachers and Bible teachers from other parts of the Body of Christ and throughout the nations to speak to us as well.

I am so grateful for these Bible teachers. I praise God for Billy Graham, who has spent his life ministering the truth of the gospel that "God so loved the world that he gave his only son" to a world audience. Evangelism is paramount in the Lord's economy; without evangelists we can easily get so caught up in our own life that we forget about the Lord's priorities.

Nearly everywhere I travel, Bible teacher Joyce Meyer can be seen and heard teaching the Bible on television. I am so grateful to the Lord for Joyce and many like her who teach the uncompromising Word of God. If we only listen to those who teach the Bible from our own camp or denomination or local church, we may not receive the whole guidance of God. Pastors who frown on those within their congregations receiving Bible teaching from the Body of Christ at large are hindering them from receiving the whole counsel of God. No single church or denomination has all of the truth.

We are all learning to grow as believers in Jesus. We need one another. Of course, all teaching must line up with the Scriptures. Let's become like the Bereans:

> Now the Bereans were of more noble character than the Thessalonians, for they received the message with great eagerness and examined the Scriptures every day to see if what Paul said was true (Acts 17:11).

With this in mind, God provides fellowship with many other believers in the greater Body of Christ—at work or school or in your community—who can help you hear from Him. We also live in a time when we can be linked with people halfway across the world with the click of an Internet connection, and many of these people may be believers in Christ who can help us hear from God.

Within the whole Body of Christ, we can find a community of believers to interact with and encourage each other to hear from God. We can find real relationship that offers a genuine connection as we serve the Lord together from various church families and denominations. God uses these believers to speak to us in ways that we might not expect.

Promise Keepers, founded in 1990, has been mightily used of God to reach more than 5 million men who have gathered in stadiums to worship the Lord together from many difference denominations. The Bible clearly speaks about the larger Body of Christ:

> The body is a unit, though it is made up of many parts; and though all its parts are many, they form one body. . . . God has arranged the parts in the body, every one of them, just as he wanted them to be. If they were all one part, where would the body be? As it is, there are many parts, but one body (1 Cor. 12:12,20).

Each year in Lancaster County, Pennsylvania, a devotional book is written by hundreds of believers and Christian leaders from the area. As thousands of these books are purchased, believers hear from the Lord each day through the devotionals written by people from many different church families and denominations.[1] We are one Body in Christ.

Biblical Preachers and God's Voice

A common way that God speaks to us is through one of His servants who is preaching under the guidance of the Holy Spirit. Biblical preachers believe that God is speaking, through His Word and His Spirit and through *them*, as they are faithful to the task of preaching God's Word.

I have often heard God speak to my spirit while listening to a preacher or teacher expounding God's Word, and it became alive to me at that moment. Preachers help us hear what God is saying. When I get the opportunity, I like to visit different churches and learn from preachers who love Jesus but are not necessarily from my Christian tradition.

Romans 10:14 shows Paul's concern for those who cannot call on the name of the Lord because no one has told them about Him:

> How, then, can they call on the one they have not believed in? And how can they believe in the one of whom they have not heard? And how can they hear without someone *preaching* to them?

Without someone preaching the good news, the lost have less chance of hearing God's voice. Although salvation is available to everyone who calls on Christ, if they have not heard of Him, how can they call on Him? Someone has to tell them, and no one will be told unless there is a preacher.

When God's servants preach under the anointing of the Holy Spirit, God is making Himself known, and we must listen to what is being said. God has revealed preaching as His way of making Himself known. Titus 1:3 says that God "manifested His Word through preaching."

John Stott wrote, "It is God's speech that makes our speech necessary. We must speak what he has spoken. Hence the paramount obligation to preach." He goes on to state that this obligation is unique to Christianity. "Only Christian preachers claim to be heralds of good news from God, and dare to think of themselves as his ambassadors or representatives who actually utter oracles of God."[2]

Throughout the Bible, from the prophets to the apostles, preaching is given a central place. Godly messengers proclaimed God's message publicly by saying, "This is what God says." Through preaching, God reveals Himself. We can hear Him by listening to what He has to say through godly preachers who preach in our local church, another church in our city, on the Internet or television or through those who have written the spiritual truths the Lord has given them in books.

Christian Books and God's Voice

Almost everyone can name one or more books that have changed their lives and helped them understand God in greater ways. I am no exception. I grew up in an Anabaptist church. But that is not where I learned about leading people to Christ. I learned this from a book written by a Baptist. I learned about the work of the Holy Spirit from a book I read by David Wilkerson, an Assembly of God preacher who started Teen Challenge. I learned about healthy family life from a book written by a Lutheran pastor. And I learned about discipleship from the writings of the Navigators and Campus Crusade for Christ. Books are a powerful means to change our worldview and wake us up to new spiritual dimensions.

The greater Body of Christ holds a place for us to grow spiritually and hear God more clearly.

Apply What You've Learned

VERSE TO REMEMBER:

*The body is a unit, though it is made up of many parts;
and though all its parts are many, they form one body.*
1 CORINTHIANS 12:12

1. How has God used a Bible teacher in the Body of Christ to speak to you?
2. How does God reveal Himself through preaching?
3. Explain how a book has opened your heart and mind to greater spiritual dimensions.

Notes
1. God Story devotional books are available at http://www.dcfi.org/House2House/One_Devotional.html.
2. John Stott, *Between Two Worlds* (Grand Rapids, MI: Wm. B. Eerdmans Publishing Co, 1982, reprinted 2000), pp. 15-16.

31

Other People

I have often heard the Lord speak to me through the counsel of others; and more times than I can count, the Lord has used my wife to speak something that God wanted to say to me. God wants us to pay attention to godly people who have consistently listened to Him and obeyed Him. These wise counselors have become familiar with God's voice and can give us godly insights that will aid us in making proper decisions.

The book of Proverbs discloses the benefits of listening to godly counselors for advice: "Where there is no counsel, the people fall; but in the multitude of counselors there is safety" (Prov. 11:14, *NKJV*). God often uses the counsel of other believers to clarify ambiguous areas or to give us the assurance that we are truly hearing from Him. These people speak "a word in due season" to help us to discern God's voice. Sometimes they can give us a word of advice that confirms what we already feel in our own spirit.

My friend Beth recalls a time when God spoke to her through another person who gave her much-needed godly counsel. Beth is a person who loves to give to others and often gets ideas for gifts and creative things to do for other people. For a period of time, however, she started to feel that her ideas were just too expensive and took too much time to implement. Some time later, during a group prayer time, a man told Beth a story that he sensed was from the Lord. He told the Bible story of the woman pouring out expensive perfume on Jesus' feet. Others complained about the wasted resource. Beth immediately knew that God was challenging her to continue to give to others as part of her giving to Him. It was worth the time and cost. Beth was grateful that someone had heard from God and challenged her to do what she knew deep inside God had called her to do. God had spoken to her through another person.

We Need Each Other

I think the reason that God uses others to help us hear His voice is to remind us that we are not self-sufficient. God placed us on Earth to interact with others and give up our self-centeredness and independence so that we can become interdependent. We need each other.

The Bible says that it is a privilege and a joy to be able to hear from God and pass that guidance on to another: "A man finds joy in giving an apt reply—and how good is a timely word!" (Prov. 15:23). I was talking recently to a friend in Canada, and he asked me for advice on decisions he was making for his future. I gave him the guidance I felt the Lord was giving to me for him. He mentioned that it was the same advice a friend from Uzbekistan gave him earlier that day. In this case, the same word was confirmed by two people, and my friend joyfully received it as a word from God.

Paul, the apostle, believed in the importance of getting a confirmation of two or three people: "Every matter must be established by the testimony of two or three witnesses" (2 Cor. 13:1). If God has spoken something to you, He will usually confirm it through yet another.

The Scriptures tell us there is power in agreement: "Again, I tell you that if two of you on earth agree about anything you ask for, it will be done for you by my Father in heaven. For where two or three come together in my name, there am I with them" (Matt. 18:19-20). God often speaks to us through agreement with others.

Sometimes people tell me, "God spoke to me, and I am not accountable to anyone, just to God." People who rarely ask for or take advice are usually dealing with pride in their life. Pride can keep us from accepting counsel from others.

Our culture may tell us to stand on our own two feet because we don't need anyone to help us make decisions. A proud person thinks that seeking advice is a sign of weakness; however, as a community of believers in Jesus, we were designed for interdependence. God speaks through other believers to the benefit of every member in the Body of Christ.

Godly Counselors

If God chooses to speak to us through others, we should humbly receive from those God chooses to use. I have found the best policy is to seek God and let Him choose how and through whom He wants to speak to us. Proverbs tells us that "plans fail for lack of counsel, but with many advisers they succeed" (Prov. 15:22).

God may speak through the counsel we receive from experts in a particular field. For example, a doctor gives me advice for maintaining a healthy body. My financial advisor gives counsel on making sound financial decisions. An editor helps me write a book, and so on.

The purpose of a "multitude of counselors" or "many advisors" is to receive a greater variety of wisdom. Obviously, we do not listen to just any person who gives us advice. The story is told of two destitute old men sitting on a park bench. One said, "I'm a man who never took advice from anybody." The other man said, "Old buddy, I'm a man who followed everybody's advice!" When we are not selective about taking advice, it could lead to our ruin.

When listening to the godly counsel of others, it is sometimes difficult to know if you have heard from God correctly or if others have heard accurately. The Bible urges us to "test the spirits" (1 John 4:1). If another believer claims to speak a word from God for you, test it. Ask God to confirm to you if it is really from Him.

If you have any doubts, go to your pastor or another proven Christian leader. These trusted leaders have traveled down the road before you, and they are examples of godly living. You can trust them for advice. Ask them to pray about it with you.

The Bible says that we should know the lives of those from whom we receive wisdom and direction: "Know those who labor among you—your leaders who are over you in the Lord and those who warn and kindly reprove and exhort you" (1 Thess. 5:12, *AMP*).

Godly counselors are people who practice what they preach and have a track record of making good decisions. A godly counselor will be able to hear God's voice and confirm what God has been speaking to you. Godly counselors are those who love the Lord. You can trust them because they bear the good spiritual fruit of living close to Jesus (see Matt. 7:15-20). Additionally, the benchmark of godly counselors is that they will be concerned about what happens after they give advice, because they care about you and want to see you succeed.

A godly counselor's goal is to give words of advice that confirm what you already feel in your own spirit, always leaving you to make the final decision based on hearing God's voice.

Apply What You've Learned

VERSE TO REMEMBER:

In a multitude of counselors there is safety.
PROVERBS 24:6, *NKJV*

1. Why do you think there is "safety in a multitude of counselors"?

2. What is the danger of seeking others' opinions before seeking God's?

3. Have you ever experienced a time when you felt God speak something to you, and it was confirmed by another person? Describe how this helped you.

32

Testimonies

Three times the book of Acts records Paul telling of his conversion. Apparently Paul knew the power of his personal story to move people closer to hearing from God for themselves. The skeptics of his day, just like today, debated the validity of the risen Jesus and that He died for their sins, but they couldn't deny Paul's personal experiences with Jesus.

In the book of Thessalonians, Paul commended the Christians for believing his testimony: "On the day he comes to be glorified in his holy people and to be marveled at among all those who have believed. This includes you, because you believed our testimony to you" (2 Thess. 1:10).

When you tell your story of how God has transformed your life, no one can argue or debate it because you are going beyond the realm of knowledge into the realm of your personal relationship with God. Your story is a powerful example of how God has worked in your life. Your testimony is your personal story of encountering the Lord and what He has done for you and in you.

Your testimony can have a real impact on others' lives. People will listen when you tell your personal story of how you came to believe in Jesus. They will not be intimidated, because they are not forced to agree or disagree with the statements you make. It is your story, and they cannot deny how you were persuaded to follow Jesus.

When you share your story with others, you should focus on the fact that God loves them and Jesus died for them, so they can be forgiven and be made new as well. Tell them of the changes the Lord has made in your life, which will give them hope for their life too.

Never be ashamed to speak for Christ: "So do not be ashamed to testify about our Lord, or ashamed of me his prisoner. But join with me in suffering for the gospel, by the power of God, who has saved us and called us to a holy life—not because of anything we have done but because of his own purpose and grace" (2 Tim. 1:8-9).

A friend and I went to pray for a man who had cancer. My friend, the man's believing wife and his daughter-in-law had been praying for his salvation for many years, but he had not received Christ. Upon entering his home, the Holy Spirit prompted me to share my personal testimony with him. About 30 minutes later, he was ready to receive Jesus Christ as the Lord of his life. God used my testimony to speak to him, and his life was changed.

As you share your testimony, you'll find that the Holy Spirit will use you to speak the truth, and others will be built up in faith. Perhaps you are afraid that someone will ask you a question you don't have the answer to. If you are unsure of the correct answer, it is appropriate to say, "I don't know, but perhaps I can ask someone who does know." None of us has all the answers. That's why the Lord placed different gifts in different people in His church. We all need each another.

Because the Lord has given all those who are His a powerful testimony, sometimes there is nothing quite like the testimony of another to get through to us. This is how it happened to me.

When I was growing up, my family went to church every Sunday in our community. When I was 11 years old, we went to an evangelistic meeting, and God convicted me of my sin. The preacher talked about eternal life and the importance of living for God and not spending eternity in hell. I remember thinking that night that I did not want to go to hell. So, I gave my life to God. I was baptized and became a church member.

I wanted to live for the Lord, but in reality, the commitment I made lasted only a few months. It wasn't long before I was living a counterfeit Christian life. When I was with my Christian friends, I acted like a Christian. When I was with my non-Christian friends, I acted like them.

Seven years later, a friend confronted me with the question, "If you were to die tonight, are you sure you would go to heaven?" I didn't know the answer. I responded, "Nobody knows that!"

My friend said, "Well, I know."

I was uncomfortable that night because I was confronted with the truth. You see, I could talk about God and the Bible, but I couldn't talk about Jesus, because I did not know Him personally. I imagined that if I did good things, somehow God would accept me.

I went home and opened my Bible. Suddenly, everything I read spoke directly to me. I read where Jesus spoke to the religious people of His day, "You hypocrites!" I was a hypocrite. I knew that even though others had viewed me as "the life of the party," when I went home, I was lonely. I was afraid that I would die without God. That night, I said, "Jesus, I give You my life. If You can use this rotten, mixed-up life, I'll serve You the rest of my life."

God took me at my word. I was born again and became a new creation in Christ! My attitudes changed. My desires changed. The way I thought changed. And the Lord used the testimony of a friend, who later became my wife, to speak to me. I am eternally grateful!

You, too, have a story to tell, and people want to hear that you have experienced the same needs they have and that Jesus Christ has met those needs in your life. In your story (your testimony), you should include not only the outward sins that bound you, but the inward needs that drove you. Your personal testimony may consist of:

- Describing the circumstance of your conversion—how you became a Christian (where, when and what happened)

- Mentioning what the need was in your life, prior to your salvation, that brought you to Christ

- Relating how your need has now been met after receiving Jesus[1]

It is important to give your testimony—your experience of your encounter with Jesus—as often as possible to as many people as possible. You have a story to tell just as the woman at the well, or the blind man, or the woman caught in adultery had a story to tell! Your story is your experience of God's kindness and power and love. You are telling what the Lord has done in your life and what God is saying about you. We know what God says about us by believing His Word. It is the truth of God's Word that sets us free.

The Bible says that one of the ways we overcome Satan is by speaking out for Christ: "They overcame him by the blood of the Lamb and by the word of their testimony" (Rev. 12:11). Why can't Satan stand against our story? I believe it is because the power and forgiveness of God is in our story. There is spiritual power released against the powers of darkness when we testify how the Lord has changed and is changing our lives.

Start telling your story today!

Apply What You've Learned

VERSE TO REMEMBER:

They overcame him by the blood of the Lamb and by the word of their testimony.
REVELATION 12:11

1. How can you hear God through someone else's testimony?
2. Why is Satan silenced when we tell our testimony?
3. Share your testimony with someone today!

Note

1. Larry Kreider, *What Does It Mean to Be a Real Christian?* (Lititz, PA: House to House Publications, 2007), pp. 19-20.

33

Authorities

We live in a culture where submission to authority is not popular. People have bumper stickers that say "Question Authority." Granted, authority has been abused. Many of us have felt let down by parents, pastors and presidents. But God's kingdom is based on recognition of an authority structure.

Whether we'll admit it or not, we all long for the structure of proper authority. We love to watch football games or action movies where a team of people works together under a strong leader to accomplish great things. The centurion in Matthew 8:9 understood the nature of authority when he said, "I am a man under authority, and I have men under my authority." This kind of authority brings protection and accountability to everyone. It also puts us in a place to be able to hear from God.

Because the Genesis account of mankind's fall had its source in rebellion, and rebellion disrupts authority, we will have trouble hearing God's voice if we rebel against the authorities God has set in place for us. If we respect and honor these authorities, we open a channel of communication with God. Authorities help us with the timing of the Lord's direction, and God uses them to help build character in our life.

All authority comes from God. Since the beginning of time, God has ruled and upheld the universe with His authority. God delegated authority to His Son: "All authority has been given to Me in heaven and on earth" (Matt. 28:18, *NKJV*, see also 1 Pet. 2:13); and under the authority of Jesus are levels of earthly authority.

God carries out His authority through four God-ordained human institutions: government, parents, employers and church leaders. When we honor and respect teachers, employers, police officers, our church leadership and our parents, we are honoring Christ.

Submitting to those who are in authority actually protects us. For example, if we disobey the speed limit, we could be killed or we could kill someone else. If a parent tells a child not to play with matches, and he disobeys, there could be the loss of a home or the loss of life. It would not be the parents' fault or God's fault; the child simply disobeyed the authority that was placed in his life. He moved out from under the umbrella of God's protection.

Rebellion Affects Our Hearing

Peter urged the Christian believers to "be subject for the Lord's sake to every human institution" (Rom. 13:1-2). If we rebel against any of these established human institutions, we violate God's divine authority. We are going to have trouble hearing God's voice if rebellion and disrespect cloud our lives.

This is not to say that we cannot question authority if the questions are asked in a spirit of humility and respect.

The Bible says that the "powers that be" are ordained by God.

> Everyone must submit himself to the governing authorities, for there is no authority except that which God has established. The authorities that exist have been established by God. Consequently, he who rebels against the authority is rebelling against what God has instituted, and those who do so will bring judgment on themselves (Isa. 14:14, *NKJV*).

This Scripture does not mean that God endorses everything that civil governments do; but because God puts governments in place, we should submit to governmental leaders out of respect for God. Although this Scripture is talking about submitting to governing authorities, it applies to all authorities in our life. If I am careless in obeying earthly authority, I place myself in a position of disobedience to the ultimate authority that stands behind the earthly—God's authority. We apply this when we remind our children that if they do not learn to respect their parents, they will have trouble respecting anyone or anything else.

Submitting to Authorities Protects

Having an attitude of submission toward the authorities God has placed in our life will protect us from many mistakes. I was talking to a new believer who was lamenting about a parole officer giving him input he did not like. I explained to him that God probably was speaking through that parole officer and using her words to speak into his life. An attitude of submission is also a protection against the influence of the devil. The nature of the devil is rebellious and deceitful. Lucifer fell from heaven because he said, "I will be like the Most High" (Isa. 14:14). He refused to submit to God's authority. Whenever we allow an attitude of rebellion into our lives, we are beginning to be motivated by the enemy, which leads us to sin against God.

God's Guidance Through Authorities

Submitting to the authority the Lord has placed in our life often provides guidance for us to know God's will. As a young man, my parents asked me to break off my relationship with certain ungodly friends. At the time, I did not appreciate what they were telling me. I felt controlled. But in retrospect, I am thankful to God for giving me the grace to submit to their authority. I realize now that it saved me from having my life shipwrecked. God spoke to me through the authority of my parents.

Joseph, in the Old Testament, submitted to the authority of the jailer, even though he was falsely imprisoned. The Lord later raised him up as prime minister for the nation.

Jesus Himself submitted to His heavenly Father every day. He said, "for I seek not to please myself but him who sent me" (Acts 5:29). Jesus was committed to walking in submission to His heavenly Father's authority. Jesus did nothing of His own initiative, but only that which was initiated by His heavenly Father. He also spent the early years of His life submitting to His earthly father in the carpentry shop.

What to Do When Authority Is Misguided

This brings us to a very important question. "What should I do if the authority in my life is wrong?" The Bible makes it clear that if any person in authority in our life requires us to sin, we must obey God and not man (see Dan. 1:8,12-13). If the authorities in our life are asking us to cheat, steal, lie or sin in any way, we must obey the living God! The Early Church leaders were told by the religious leaders of their day to stop proclaiming Jesus as Lord. They could not obey those orders; however, they still maintained a spirit and attitude of honor toward the religious leaders.

What if we believe the godly authority in our life is not sinning, but simply making a mistake? Philippians 4:6 tells us to make an appeal. "Do not be anxious about anything, but in everything, by prayer and petition, with thanksgiving, present your requests to God."

First of all, we need to appeal to God. We should pray, making known our requests and concerns as we appeal to Him as our ultimate authority. This sets a precedent for appeal to the delegated authorities in our life.

Daniel and his friends, in the Old Testament, appealed to the authority in their lives and asked that they be allowed to eat only certain foods. The Lord honored their appeal to authority and blessed them with health, wisdom, literary skill and supernatural revelation (see Dan. 1:11-17).

Nehemiah appealed to the king to take a trip to Jerusalem (see Neh. 1). His appeal to the authority in his life, made in an attitude of submission, caused the king to grant his request. Nehemiah's attitude and obedience made it possible for him to hear the voice of God regarding the wall to be built around Jerusalem.

An attitude of love and submission toward those God has placed in authority in our life releases us to hear Him speak. God's intention is to use the authorities He has placed to help mold and structure our life for His good. In many cases, listening to these authorities opens the door for us to hear God's voice.

Apply What You've Learned

VERSE TO REMEMBER:

Everyone must submit himself to the governing authorities,
for there is no authority except that which God has established.
The authorities that exist have been established by God.
ROMANS 13:1

1. What often happens when we rebel against authority?

2. Have you ever appealed to your pastor, parent, employer or the government because they were wrong? Give examples.

3. Tell how honoring and respecting authority has released you to hear from God.

Section Six

SPIRITUAL DISCIPLINES AND TAKING ACTION

34

Taking a Step of Faith

People often ask me, "How do I find the destiny the Lord has called me to? I just do not have a complete picture of what God is saying." Some people spend many years waiting to hear a voice from heaven or they wait until they receive supernatural direction. Many never receive it.

I believe that we must step out in faith, and God will lead us from there. It is hard to steer a car that is not moving. You may need to be moving if you want God to show you which way to go. The Lord tells us, "A man's mind plans his way, but the Lord directs his steps and makes them sure" (Prov. 16:9, *RSV*). God leads one step at a time; and if you take one step forward, and it's the wrong way, He will let you know before you go too far. Step out in faith and find which doors God will open for you and which ones He will close.

Baby Steps

If you've seen the movie *What About Bob?* you will remember that a therapy patient, who fears everything and anything, is initially advised by his therapist to take "baby steps" to learn to function normally. The comical story takes us through the many antics of Bob as he learns to take those first steps.

Taking small, slow steps at first will prevent you from falling too hard if you are wrong! You can stick a toe in the water to test the temperature, so to speak. When you take one small step of faith, and God opens a door, then you can take another step. If He closes the door, then you back off. Try another direction or wait awhile; but always keep praying and then step out again.

Even the parents of Jesus had to make some adjustments in their direction until they had it right. An angel of the Lord appeared to Joseph in a dream and told him to take baby Jesus back to Israel. So Joseph headed in that direction; but on the way, he was frightened to hear that the new king was Herod's son, who also wanted to kill Jesus.

Then in another dream, Joseph was warned not to go to Judea, so they went to Galilee instead and lived in Nazareth (see Matt. 2:19-23). Joseph and Mary were not sure what steps they should take, but they took one step at a time.

The Lord knows that He could overwhelm us by revealing His whole plan at once. It's so big that we might be frightened and not take the first step. Consequently, He leads us one step at a time so that we can handle it.

God doesn't push us out into the cold with only a map in our hands. He leads us by providing His Holy Spirit to guide us. He wants us to keep our eyes on Him, and then follow alongside Him step by step.

When I read in Acts that Paul and Silas were trying to go into Bithynia and were being prevented by the Spirit, it was life changing for me. Without knowing the full scope of God's plan, Paul and Silas obeyed the Spirit's voice and went in another direction. It turned out that the Holy Spirit had greater plans for them, which they did not recognize at the time (see Acts 16:7). But because they were moving, God could more easily guide them.

Taking this biblical example, I was no longer afraid to take steps of faith in my own life. I knew that I could trust the Lord to keep me from going to places that were not in His perfect plan for me. I could trust Him to lead me with His divine direction and, in faith, step into God's plans.

Some of God's people spend their lives in so much fear of making a mistake that they never do anything. There are times when it is much better to do something rather than continue to do nothing. Without faith it is impossible to please God (see Heb. 11:6). We cannot trust in our own abilities, but we can trust in His ability, because Christ lives in us.

Jesus honored whatever His Father said, no matter what the personal cost, and indeed it cost His life. We will not hear the Lord's voice clearly if we only listen to God when what He says is not going to cost us anything, or if we only listen when He tells us what we want to hear. Our natural inclination is to manipulate things to work the way we want them to work. But we must be willing to lay aside our own desires or we may miss a clear word from the Lord.

We need to be open to messages that God may send through people who love us and are praying for us. God wants us to stay humble and always be ready to hear from Him in whatever way He chooses to speak.

Position Yourself to Hear

Learning to discern God's voice takes effort on our part. The Lord wants us to take the time to listen as we open our hearts to hear. He wants us to become increasingly familiar with His voice as our relationship deepens with Him. The more often we meet with God in prayer and talk to Him, the clearer His voice becomes.

The Bible instructs us to make a concerted effort to meet with the Lord, thereby placing ourselves in a position to hear from Him: "Then you will call upon me and come and pray to me, and I will listen to you. You will seek me and find me when you seek me with all your heart" (Jer. 29:12-13). God wants us to acknowledge Him in our life (see Prov. 3:6). If we acknowledge a friend, we talk to Him, express our appreciation for Him and recognize His presence in our life.

Imagine your friends not acknowledging your presence when you are together. You try to talk to them, but they completely ignore you. In fact, they talk right over you as if you were not even there. That is how we treat the Lord if we are not acknowledging Him moment by moment. If we do not recognize God's presence in our daily life, it is little wonder that we have trouble hearing from Him.

Tune In

Although we may wish that God would send a glowing 10-foot angel to reveal God's will to us so that we have no doubt it is His voice we are hearing, I believe that He often teaches us through our stumbling attempts of trial and error as we take steps of faith.

About 20 years ago, my father told me that he thought I would someday become a writer. At that point in my life, becoming a writer was not on my radar screen. But the Lord used my father to plant the seed in my memory. A few years later, when I was encouraged to write the story of how God led us to start a church in rural Pennsylvania, which grew to more than 2,000 people and sent missionaries to the nations, I decided to at least give it a try, and my first book, *House to House,* was eventually written. I wasn't even sure it was the right timing, but I had peace to take a step of faith. Now, 15 years and more than 20 books later, I can understand how important it was for me to take that first step.

Apply What You've Learned

VERSE TO REMEMBER:

A man's mind plans his way, but the Lord directs his steps and makes them sure.
PROVERBS 16:9, *RSV*

1. How do you place yourself in a position to hear from God?

2. Describe a time when you took one step of faith and God opened a door for you to walk through.

3. Tell of a time when you were afraid to take a step of faith. Did you hear from God?

35

Mentors and Spiritual Parents

The Christian life is about relationship with God and with one another. Many times the Lord speaks to us through these relationships. Mentoring, or a spiritual parenting relationship, opens the door for the Lord to speak through a mentor in our life. We need help to grow up spiritually. Just as natural infants cannot thrive alone, young believers need care and nurture to help them reach their potential in Christ.

A pastor friend told me that as a young believer he yearned for someone to take the time to love him, train and discipline him, and impart their wisdom to him. Although he recognized God as his Father, and he had a natural father who set an example for him, he did not have a spiritual father to lovingly disciple him and nudge him to grow in his Christian life.

He recalls, "I was left on my own until, at a Bible school, I met a loving elderly professor who asked if I could pray with him regularly. I believe this was a divine plan of God to initiate me into his family. Our weekly prayer meetings soon took the form of a father-son relationship. I loved it. I was able to open up. I felt like I was being born again, this time with a sense of security, love and deep humility. God became a friend, not just a father who watched my actions to find a reason to chastise, correct or rebuke me."

This pastor had finally found someone who would make an investment into his life and challenge him to maturity. This personal care helped him hear from God and trust God's faithful involvement in his life.

Paul, the apostle, told the Corinthian believers that they needed spiritual parents to help them grow up: "Even though you have ten thousand guardians in Christ, you do not have many fathers, for in Christ Jesus I became your father through the gospel. Therefore I urge you to imitate me. For this reason I am sending to you Timothy, my son whom I love, who is faithful in the Lord. He will remind you of my way of life in Christ Jesus" (1 Cor. 4:15-17).

Paul had been like a father to the Corinthians and had their best interests at heart. He wanted them not only to rely on instructors or teachers to help them grow, but to also look for spiritual parents, like himself, who would be willing to pass on a legacy from their own lives as they poured what they had into their spiritual children.

Paul goes on to say that he would send Timothy to the Corinthian church. As a spiritual father, Paul had faithfully trained Timothy. Now Timothy was ready to impart his spiritual fatherhood to the Corinthian church. Christian believers need to see spiritual parenting modeled so that they can be equipped to pass on a legacy to the next generation of believers. With this example, they can produce their own spiritual sons and daughters. This kind of relationship of training and equipping is a spiritual investment that will continue to multiply.

The measure of greatness of a spiritual parent is his level of servanthood and love. Spiritual fathers and mothers are in a place to help spiritual sons and daughters negotiate the obstacles of their spiritual journey, hear from God and reach their God-given potential. A spiritual son or daughter needs to see his or her parents in action in everyday life as they love and gently encourage their children to hear from God.

Communication Gap

I believe that God desires to see intergenerational families working together and passing on a blessing from one generation to the next. In today's society, we see the effects of parents being alienated from their children. In the book of Malachi, the prophet said that when the hearts of fathers and children are estranged from one another, a curse strikes the land (see Mal. 4:5-6). While this curse takes various forms in society, it also affects the church. Satan wants to intimidate the older folk and distract the younger. He uses tools of suspicion and indifference to drive a wedge between them.

But where there is a peaceful coexistence of intergenerational families, a blessing is passed on from one generation to the next. When the hearts of the children and the fathers are turned toward each other rather than against each other, an environment is created that allows individuals to give their best. In this environment, they can hear God speak more clearly.

Betty, in her fifties, started to mentor Holly during a time of deep need in Holly's life. Holly was a 27-year-old mother, yet she was a child crying out from within a woman's body. During their mentoring relationship, Betty visited Holly every week and called her several times a week. They read helpful books together and Betty taught Holly how to cook, something she had never learned growing up. Holly recalled:

> Betty practiced what she preached. She helped me to hear from God by her example. God spoke through Betty as she faithfully mentored me. Trust is a very important part of spiritual parenting. I had trust issues in my life, and she never betrayed my trust or gossiped. If she made a mistake, she humbled herself and admitted it. A spiritual parent doesn't have to be perfect, just real and honest.

Although Betty and Holly came from very different upbringings, and didn't always agree on things, the love of Jesus brought them together. Holly's life was forever impacted by this spiritual parenting relationship that helped her get to know God and hear His voice.

Training Their Ears to Hear

In my book *Authentic Spiritual Mentoring,* I explain that spiritual parents must teach their protégés to hear from God because they will only grow to maturity as they learn to hear and discern God's voice for themselves.

> To hear God's voice clearly, we must have a growing love relationship with God and trust Him. It's that simple. The better we get to know God, the better we will recognize His voice. On the other hand, we need to share with our protégé that everyone at one time or another struggles to hear God's voice. We want to do what the Lord wants us to do and we know we serve a living God who speaks to us, yet we all struggle when we do not hear as clearly as we would like. Despite our trouble hearing, God wants to speak to us even more than we desire to hear from Him. He often teaches us through our stumbling attempts of trial and error.[1]

Spiritual parents and mentors always have the goal of developing their protégés to be ready to fly out of the nest, so to speak, because they believe in them and have confidence in them. When mentors help protégés discover and develop their gifts and hear from God for themselves, the protégés, who are now controlled and energized by the Holy Spirit, can go out and teach others what they have learned so that another generation of spiritual parents can be equipped. The multiplication potential is limitless.

I am grateful to the Lord that after many years when I did not have a spiritual father and mentor in my life, the Lord provided spiritual mentors to speak into my life—men older and wiser and with much more life experience. Over and over again, I have found that their counsel is filled with wisdom from the Lord. The Lord speaks through spiritual mentors.

Apply What You've Learned

VERSE TO REMEMBER:

Even though you have ten thousand guardians in Christ, you do not have many fathers. . . . Therefore I urge you to imitate me.
1 CORINTHIANS 4:15-16

1. How has a mentor helped you hear God's voice?
2. What is the benefit of having a spiritual parent?
3. What's holding you back from becoming a mentor to someone?

Note
1. Larry Kreider, *Authentic Spiritual Mentoring* (Ventura, CA: Regal Books, 2008).

36

Coaching and Spiritual Direction

A coach is someone who wants to see you win. This definition does not change, whether we are referring to a sports coach or a life coach. A coach wants to win the game, whatever "the game" is, and he does everything in his power to help you achieve that win! A coach, in general, is one who applies strategies and tactics so that the outcome can be one of triumph, breakthrough and a fulfillment of the dream.

Similar to a mentor, a life coach is a person who helps people achieve their goals and dreams. A life coach helps a person clarify goals and develop strategies toward achieving those goals. "Unlike a counselor or mentor, a coach rarely offers advice. Coaching does not include the given solution for the problem but will energize the coachee to solve the problem."[1] Coaching is really a way of helping us make the best use of our resources.

In his book *Transformational Coaching*, my friend Dr. Joseph Umidi describes a type of coaching that aims to accomplish so much more than simply making good use of our resources.

> I am thankful for the people who have helped me understand my own voice, coached me to knowing what I wanted to do, but I am certainly glad I did not stop there. Coaching that is short of transformational only puts us in touch with ourselves, many times a self that is on the throne, a self that we can too easily idolize, a self that can become an imposing taskmaster itself. But thank God for transformational coaches who understand that God's voice fulfills our voices, and God's heart awakens our hearts to a fulfillment that is not only eternal, but makes this side of heaven so much more significant.[2]

He says that "true transformation comes from hearing [God's] voice and then finding our voice and destiny despite any circumstances beyond our control. His voice resonates in our hearts and confirms in us that He is the right source to look for the right answers for each of us."[3]

The Right Questions

A key to effective coaching is the art of asking the right questions. When we are properly coached, we usually end up finding God's direction and hearing His voice clearly as we answer the strategic questions our coach asks us.

A coach listens to God's dream in us and helps us match the dream with the way God expresses Himself through us. We are all unique, and we all have to build on the resources and strengths God has given us to get where we want to go. A coach helps us develop that dream as we hear from God for ourselves in virtually any area of life: our spiritual life, business, career, family, health, personal growth, intimacy and financial development.

Danail Tenev, a pastor and nationally known musician in Bulgaria, told me how his life changed through being coached by his friend and coach Les Brickman. "It was so freeing," he told me. "Les did not tell me what I should be doing, but he helped me find what God had already placed on my heart by asking the right questions."

Coaching and spiritual direction (which we will look at next) are similar. While coaching is more about overcoming some obstacle or moving from a "stuck place" into a place of being able to hear God, spiritual direction is about deepening your spiritual life as you learn to hear God speak clearly. Both focus on your inner being. Both help you listen and ask questions so that you can listen to God in your daily life.

Spiritual Direction

Spiritual direction takes place when help is given by one Christian to another to enable the individual to pay close attention to God's personal communication and grow in intimacy with God. The director helps the person explore a deeper relationship with God, asking, "Where is God in this experience?" He or she listens to the nuances of a person's life, gathering the many threads together and inviting the Spirit of God to reveal patterns, movements and counter-movements that affect one's spiritual life.

To Protestant ears, spiritual direction may sound like a new idea. But the practice of spiritual direction is an ancient one going back to the fourth and fifth centuries A.D. It is rooted in the ancient experience and teachings of the desert mystics and powerhouse saints like Ignatius, Benedict, Teresa of Avila, and others. Spiritual direction has been particularly strong within Roman Catholic and Orthodox religious orders for quite some time. More recently, Protestant traditions have begun to recover it more fully. Because the term "spiritual direction" is rather new to Protestant vocabulary, let's broadly define this practice of accompanying people on a spiritual journey as the Christian disciplines, which include prayer, silence and solitude, discernment, writing in a journal, and others are explored.

David Benner says that spiritual direction is "a prayer process in which a person seeking help in cultivating a deeper personal relationship with God meets with another for prayer and conversation that is focused on increasing awareness of God in the midst of life experiences and facilitating surrender to God's will."[4]

The spiritual director helps the directee listen to the Holy Spirit for the benefit of becoming more attuned to God. As they meet, they are dedicated to listening to God's ways and desires. They meet to listen to the Holy Spirit and to each other for the benefit of the directee. As humans, we are often tempted to project our own personal heart's desires as being the will of God. Consequently, we may need a guide or director to help us distinguish between the voice of God and other voices. We can benefit from someone to encourage us as we sort out our ideas and feelings and invite God to be present as we do so.

In brief, spiritual direction normally works like this: a seeker in search of deeper meaning in his or her ordinary life meets regularly with a director for conversation about whatever the seeker wants to address in the context of faith. Spiritual directors emphasize that they don't actually "direct" or tell the seeker what to do or how to fix problems. Instead spiritual direction involves listening with compassion as sacred stories are shared. All directors, regardless of their tradition, agree that the Holy Spirit is the true Director.

Varieties of Spiritual Companionship

Sometimes it is not easy to differentiate between spiritual direction, mentoring and discipling, because they share similarities. The primary difference is that a spiritual director asks the question of where God is in the experience and what He is saying. There is no giving advice, little to no teaching or giving information, and no problem solving.

Counseling and mentoring often focus more on solving a problem or finding a solution. Most models of counseling and mentoring assume that the counselee is willing to change and will rely on training or guidance in order to make a decision to behave differently. Spiritual direction is different.

In spiritual direction, we are intentionally giving ourselves to God as both our beginning and end goal. We are not seeking change per se, we are seeking to trust God and not control our own life. We are seeking to have a greater awareness of God's presence with us and explore what it means to abide. We are learning to be more like Mary of Bethany who sat at Jesus' feet (see Luke 10:38-40). It's about the experience of being with God, not a theology or doctrine.

The Discipline of Spiritual Direction

In summary, spiritual direction is a discipline in which, with the help of another, you try to listen to your own heart and to God's. It is a place to talk about what you are thinking as you give God your full attention and seek to discern what He is saying. You can be yourself and ask God to be part of the conversation as you talk to another person about how you are responding to God or resisting God in your journey through life. Usually the agenda of spiritual direction is to have no agenda except to be open to God as you meet with your spiritual director and ask the Holy Spirit to be the real director.

Whether it is in coaching or spiritual direction, you will learn to listen, share and ask questions to help you discover God's will for you and help you take the next steps in God's plan as you learn to hear His voice.

Apply What You've Learned

VERSE TO REMEMBER:

Mary . . . sat at the Lord's feet listening to what he said.
LUKE 10:39

1. How does coaching help an individual make the best use of his or her resources?

2. Explain the difference between coaching and spiritual direction.

3. What does an effective coach do? What does an effective spiritual director do?

Notes
1. "Coaching," Wikipedia. http://en.wikipedia.org/wiki/Coaching (accessed September 2007).
2. Dr. Joseph Umidi, *Transformational Coaching* (xulonpress.com, 2005), pp. 20-21.
3. Ibid.
4. David Benner, *Sacred Companions* (Downers Grove, IL: InterVarsity Press, 2002), p. 94.

37

Fasting

"Do you want to super-size it?" "Be sure to save room for dessert."
Everywhere we turn, we are encouraged to indulge. Television commercials, billboards and the far-too-convenient fast-food restaurants in our neighborhood do not make it easy to deny ourselves.

What is fasting, and why should we deny ourselves by practicing this spiritual discipline? When we fast, we are abstaining from daily nourishment for a period of time. We "starve" our body in order to feed our spirit. The essence of a fast is self-denial in order to turn our thoughts to God.

We can hear God's voice more clearly when we fast, because we find in Him sustenance beyond food. That's probably what makes fasting so powerful. Fasting is not about denying ourselves to impress God. But as we deny ourselves and focus on God, our faith deepens and becomes more powerful. This heightened level of faith pushes back the strongholds of the enemy more effectively than verbal prayer alone. When we fast and intercede, we pray and expect God to answer. When prayer and fasting is combined, powerful things happen.

One of our church's small groups witnessed first-hand the power of prayer and fasting. A woman in their group could not kick a drug habit. They had been praying for Sarah for quite some time. Finally, the small group said, "Lord, we just really want her to follow after You; do whatever it takes, Lord!" They initiated a three-day prayer and fast. Many in the group had never been on a fast before, but they fasted and prayed nonetheless. On the third day, Sarah was getting high with a friend, and they started talking about God. As Sarah drove home that day, the Lord spoke clearly to her spirit. She heard Him say, "I am the way."

A bit unnerved, Sarah immediately drove to her sister's apartment. She said, "I don't know what just happened exactly, but I think God spoke to me and said He was 'the way.' What is this? What's it all about?" As they began to talk, Sarah gave her life to Jesus, flushed all drugs down the drain, got baptized and testified in the small group of the goodness of the Lord. Because a team of Christians had circled around a broken-hearted sister by prayer and fasting, God moved in a powerful way.

In Mark 9, Jesus healed a boy with an evil spirit. The disciples asked Jesus afterwards, "Why could we not cast him [the evil spirit] out?" Jesus replied, "This kind can come out only by prayer and fasting" (Mark 9:29, *NKJV*). Jesus was challenging His disciples to maintain a life of prayer and fasting so that their faith remained firm.

> Jesus does not mean that a time of prayer was necessary before this kind of evil spirit could be driven out. Rather, a principle is implied here: where there is little faith, there is little prayer. Where there is much prayer [and fasting], founded on true commitment to God and His Word, there is much faith. Had the disciples been maintaining as Jesus did, a life of prayer, they could have dealt successfully with this case.[1]

Maintaining a life of prayer and fasting is paramount to hearing from God. Many times my associates and I have heard the voice of God in a significant way while engaged in a season of fasting. One associate, who gets numerous speaking engagements, makes the decision about which ones to accept during a time of fasting. It is especially important for him to know which engagements to accept when extensive traveling is involved. He makes the final decision during times of fasting because fasting sharpens his hearing.

Fasting is not optional for Christians who are serious about their walk with God. One time, as Jesus was teaching on prayer and fasting, He used the term, "When you fast" (Matt. 6:16) and went on and made His point. Notice, He did not say, "If you fast." Jesus knew that fasting would open up a whole new realm of revelation for Christians and make it easier for them to hear the voice of the Holy Spirit. In addition to increasing our capacity to receive from the Lord, fasting has a way of quieting all the background noise of life so that we can tune in to His voice.

In the book of Acts, we find the Early Church receiving direction from the Lord as they were fasting. In Antioch, there was a group of church leaders who were worshiping the Lord and fasting when the Holy Spirit spoke to them about commissioning Barnabas and Paul and sending them on a trip to preach the gospel (see Acts. 13:3). This trip later became known as Paul's first missionary trip that took Christianity to areas that previously had not heard the gospel.

On this trip, Paul and Barnabas experienced many miracles, saw a large number of new converts and planted churches. When it was time to appoint leaders for those churches, how do you think they heard from God about who the leaders should be? It was through prayer and fasting (see Acts 14:23).

If you are considering marriage, changing jobs, changing careers or making other significant life decisions, it is to your advantage to include prayer with fasting in your decision-making process.

I love the story of Daniel. He had fasted for a period of three weeks when an angel appeared to him and said, "Since the first day that you set your mind to gain understanding . . . I have come in response. . . . I have come to explain to you what will happen" (Dan. 10:12,14). Daniel was asking the Lord a question, and the answer came as he was fasting. I call this receiving the missing piece of the puzzle. God showed Moses the pattern for the tabernacle on the mountain during fasting. When Queen Esther instructed her Jewish brethren to fast for three days and nights before she appeared before the king to plead for their lives, God answered by giving her favor with the king. The Bible is filled with examples of godly men and women who received direction from the Lord as a result of fasting.

Although I believe that we are all called to fast at certain times, we must avoid legalistic approaches to fasting. God gives grace for some individuals to fast for longer periods of time and others for shorter times. If you have never fasted before, ask God for His grace to experience the blessing of fasting.

Many people ask about the "correct" way to fast. Apart from having the right heart attitude, there really isn't a perfect formula. You can skip a meal, have only liquids for several days, or give up sweets. The point is that the absence of food makes us constantly more dependent on God and more open to His Spirit.

Some Christians fast for just a few meals or for one day each week. Others go for the longer fasts of weeks at a time. Be sure to drink water, especially if you are fasting for more than a day or two. There are many good books that can give a balanced approach to biblical fasting.[2]

We know it is God's will for us to fast, so we can trust that He will honor our obedience as we seek His voice through prayer and fasting. Genuine fasting puts things in proper focus and will always cause us to examine our heart to make sure everything is right with Him.

Apply What You've Learned

VERSE TO REMEMBER:

But when you fast, put oil on your head and wash your face, so that it will not be obvious to men that you are fasting, but only to your Father, who is unseen; and your Father, who sees what is done in secret, will reward you.
MATTHEW 6:17-18

1. How do prayer and fasting go hand in hand?

2. When should prayer be accompanied by fasting?

3. Give some examples when the Lord spoke to you through your times of prayer and fasting. (If you have never fasted while praying, see footnote 2.)

Notes
1. Donald Stamps, ed., *The Full Life Study Bible* (Grand Rapids, MI: Zondervan Publishing House, 1992).
2. Recommended books on fasting: Bill Bright, *The Transforming Power of Fasting and Prayer: Personal Accounts of Spiritual Renewal* (Orlando, FL: NewLife Publications, 1997); Elmer L. Towns, *Fasting for Spiritual Breakthrough* (Ventura, CA: Regal Books, 1996).

38

A Sabbath Rest

In the Old Testament, the fourth commandment says "Remember the Sabbath day by keeping it holy" (Exod. 20:8). Keeping the weekly Sabbath day (Saturday) was a special covenant between God and the Jews. There were great blessings for those who kept it and severe penalties for those who dishonored it. But this is not the kind of sabbath we are talking about in this chapter. In the New Testament, the apostle Paul tells us there is a "sabbath rest" for the people of God.

> There remains, then, a Sabbath-rest for the people of God; for anyone who enters God's rest also rests from his own work, just as God did from his. Let us, therefore, make every effort to enter that rest, so that no one will fall by following their example of disobedience (Heb. 4:9-11).

Entering into a sabbath rest is an *attitude of rest* that refreshes us. It is a kind of rest where we cease from our own efforts and rely entirely on God. This is why Paul declares, "Not I, but Christ. I no longer live, but Christ lives in me" (Gal. 2:20). This was also the secret of the life of Jesus, who said, "It is the Father who dwells in me who does the work" (John 14:10). "The Son can do nothing by himself" (John 5:19).

Walk Daily in His Rest

If, as a Christian, you learn that "it is God who works in you both to will and to do of his good pleasure" (Phil. 2:13), you are ceasing from dependence on your own activity. You have learned to depend on the activity of God who dwells within. That is fulfilling the true Sabbath as you walk daily in His rest.

To walk with God is to lead a life of devotion to Him. We all know what it means for two friends to walk together engaged in close and intimate conversation. And true friends love to get together whenever they can, as they build their relationship in a setting without being bombarded by the cares of life. Every August, LaVerne and I go to the beach in Florida alone. It is our favorite week of the year together. Having a devoted relationship with someone is an adventure that is full of surprises. These extended times alone with our heavenly Father open the door for us to hear His voice more clearly.

We all need a Sabbath rest—the kind of rest that involves ceasing from our own efforts and relying entirely on God. Sabbath rest comes from a person—Jesus Christ. If you have accepted Jesus as your Lord and Savior and are depending on Him alone for salvation, then you have rested from your own work. You are trusting in His finished work and you are experiencing the Sabbath rest that God wants you to have. You can live every day in the freedom and blessings of Christ's finished work as you tune in to His voice.

His yoke is easy and His burden is light (see Matt. 11:28-30). Make sure you are only carrying His burden, not self-made burdens or the burdens and expectations of others. When we live moment by moment at rest with Him, we can hear His voice so much more clearly.

Extended Times of Rest

A Sabbath rest not only involves walking daily in God's rest and care, but it can also involve taking extended times away from routine where the Lord directs us to come to a quiet place and get some rest. In resting, we can hear His voice so much more clearly. God created the earth and all of its inhabitants in six days, then rested on the seventh day. Jesus regularly took time away from the business of life to rest and get refreshed.

> The apostles gathered around Jesus and reported to him all they had done and taught. Then, because so many people were coming and going that they did not even have a chance to eat, he said to them, "Come with me by yourselves to a quiet place and get some rest." So they went away by themselves in a boat to a solitary place (Mark 6:30-33).

During times of rest the Lord can clearly speak to us because we are unencumbered with all of the details of life. God so often speaks to me when I take Sabbath time away from my busy schedule. I block off time on a regular basis to go to the mountains to pray, rest and listen to God. Taking a Sabbath rest allows us to slow down and listen. Often the noise of a busy life is so loud that it's necessary to take times of Sabbath away from the hustle and bustle to just be quiet and listen to the still, small voice of the Lord.

Many of the dramatic life changes I have made throughout my life came from what I heard the Lord tell me during a time away for rest and sabbatical. In my book *The Cry for Spiritual Fathers and Mothers*, I describe how God led me to take one much-needed Sabbath rest:

During the spring of 1992, I was ready to quit. I felt misunderstood, and I was not sure if it was worth all the hassle. I told LaVerne one day, "If I get kicked in the head one more time (figuratively speaking), I don't know if I can get up again."

As the senior leader of our church, I was frustrated, exhausted and overworked. God had given me a vision to be involved in building the underground church, but in the last few years, we had strayed from that original vision. My immaturity as a leader, lack of training and my own inability to communicate clearly the things that God was showing me led to frustration. In a misguided attempt to please everyone, I was listening to dozens of voices that seemed to be giving conflicting advice and direction. I felt unable to get back on track. I was tired and was encouraged to take a sabbatical.

It was on that sabbatical that the Lord gave me new direction. I am grateful to the Lord that he gave me the grace to continue and to believe again. Today, I am so fulfilled as the Lord has placed me back on his wall of service for him. Since that time, the Lord placed spiritual fathers in my life to encourage me. Knowing the incredible value of spiritual fathering has changed my life! It is my life's mission to be obedient to him to serve others and train others to become spiritual parents. I am so blessed the Lord would not allow me to quit. I am having the time of my life. I love my Savior; I love my wife; I love my family; I love the people I work with; I love what I do; it is great to be alive![1]

Let's both "enter into" and "remain in" His rest. When we cease from our own efforts and depend on the work of Jesus, we rest. When we cease from dependence on our own activity and rest in dependence upon the activity of Jesus who dwells within, we rest. That is our Sabbath rest. It may not always be easy to find a place of refuge, a place away from the telephone, fax machine, computer, radio or television. But we can always find a Sabbath rest by being in the presence of God and responding to His presence in us as we endeavor to hear His voice.

Apply What You've Learned

VERSE TO REMEMBER:

There remains, then, a Sabbath-rest for the people of God; for anyone who enters God's rest also rests from his own work, just as God did from his. Let us, therefore, make every effort to enter that rest, so that no one will fall by following their example of disobedience.
HEBREWS 4:9-11

1. Describe in our own words a Sabbath rest.

2. How can you walk daily in God's rest?

3. Tell of a time when you've taken an extended time of rest to hear from God.

Note
1. Larry Kreider, *The Cry for Spiritual Fathers and Mothers* (Lititz, PA: House to House Publications, 2000), p. 84.

39

Going Back to Where the Ax Head Fell

Sometimes hearing the voice of the Lord is like driving down the road through intense fog late at night. It is really a struggle. The painted lines become our guides. The painted line in the center of the road is symbolic of the Word of God. The most basic way that God speaks is through His Word, and we cannot go wrong by following it. The painted line at the side of the road is symbolic of the Holy Spirit who guides us and also helps us stay on track.

There are times, however, when it seems like we have entirely lost our way. We really want to obey the Lord and fulfill His will for our life, but somehow we can no longer see the painted lines on the road. What do we do then? There is a story in the Old Testament that gives us some insight.

A man was cutting down a tree by the river when his iron ax head fell into the water. An ax head was a very expensive tool, and the man desperately wanted to retrieve it because it was borrowed. He went to Elisha, a man of God, for help. Elisha asked the man where he had last seen it fall, threw a stick in the water, and it miraculously floated to the surface (see 2 Kings 6:1-6). At the same place that it was lost, the ax head reappeared!

We can learn an important lesson from this story. Whenever we have a problem with finding direction in our life, it is often helpful to go back to where we were certain we last heard the voice of the Lord clearly. If we do not go back, we may continue to flounder and be distressed. If we believe that we've lost our way spiritually, the Bible is very clear: "Remember the height from which you have fallen! Repent and do the things you did at first" (Rev. 2:5).

We must go back to where the ax head fell and remember the "height from which we have fallen"—where our love and obedience for the Lord declined. We need to acknowledge the Lord when we get off track and then repent (turn around) and go back to the last time we heard the clear, sharp, cutting-edge voice of the Lord. Then we obey.

The Lord called a young man to go far from home to a Bible school. After spending a few weeks in the school, he found himself having second thoughts about his decision. He hated the discipline, the climate—you name it. He stayed, however, when he remembered the time the Lord had clearly called him to go to that school. By being obedient, he was a recipient of the benefits, and the Lord did a tremendous work in his life.

In 1992, I began to question whether or not I was called to church leadership. Anything else looked much better than to continue on in a leadership role. However, I remembered the initial call when God called me to start a new church in 1980. This was the place the ax head had fallen for me, and I was convinced the Lord had spoken to me and given me a mandate to start the church. Knowing this gave me the confidence to go on. I knew He had not yet completed the work He had given me.

Do you get tired of your job sometimes? Perhaps you are tired of going to school or tired of your involvement in the church. Go back to the last time you knew you heard clearly from the Lord on the subject, and allow the Lord to take you from there. If you made a mistake, there is hope. That is why Jesus came in the first place, to forgive us as we acknowledge our sin and cleanse us and give us a brand-new start.

Remember the story of Jonah? He refused to obey the Lord, who told him to preach the gospel in the city of Nineveh. God got Jonah's attention by using ungodly sailors to push him into the ocean, and then prepared a great fish to swallow him alive. This certainly gave Jonah some time to think. I believe that Jonah thought back to where "the ax head fell" (where he went off-track) and quickly repented! The Lord gave him another chance and the fish spat him out on dry land. The Bible says in Jonah 3:1, "Then the word of the Lord came to Jonah a second time: 'Go to the great city of Nineveh and proclaim to it the message I give you.'" This time Jonah obeyed the word of the Lord and went to Nineveh.

As we repent before God, we can receive the word of the Lord a second time. A key question to ask ourselves is, "Have I obeyed the last thing the Lord asked me to do?"

One thing that used to cause stress in our marriage was the fact that I was constantly trying to find shortcuts whenever LaVerne and I were driving somewhere. To make matters worse, I usually got lost! To backtrack over and over again was embarrassing! I usually needed to go back to the last road I was familiar with before I could find the way.

If you find yourself on the wrong path, it is not the end of the world. The Lord is able to "restore the years that the locusts have eaten" (Joel 2:25), but going back to the place where you last heard from God is often the way to get to your destination. Is the Lord calling you back to the place where an ax head has fallen in your life, so that you can again hear His voice clearly?

Apply What You've Learned

VERSE TO REMEMBER:

Remember the height from which you have fallen!
Repent and do the things you did at first.
REVELATION 2:5

1. Describe a time when you lost your way and had to go back to where you last heard God.

2. Ask yourself this question: "Have I obeyed the last thing the Lord asked me to do?"

3. If you're off the path from God's last clear direction, what would you need to do today to get back on the path again?

DISCERNMENT AND SPIRITUAL WARFARE

40

Discernment

When I first became a committed Christian, I made the assumption from that day on that I would always hear the voice of God clearly. Wow, was I in for a shock! I had not yet learned the importance of growing in discernment.

I soon realized that I was actually hearing all kinds of voices inside my head. I also realized that some of those voices were most certainly not the voice of the Holy Spirit.

As time went on, it became clear to me that there are at least four different voices a Christian may hear within: one's own voice, the voice of others, the devil's voice and God's voice.

Your Voice

What happens when you are hearing your own voice instead of God's? The decisions you make often originate from your belief system. Mixed into your belief system are your personal feelings. This is your own voice, which includes your personal preferences and desires, such as whether or not you like pizza, whether you would rather go shopping or ride motorcycles, or whether you would eat cherry pie. These things are not a matter of right or wrong. They are personal preferences.

Sometimes we confuse our own desires with the voice of the Lord. Often our soul (our thoughts and emotions) can feel under pressure or want something so badly that we confuse it with hearing from God. We must be very careful if we are hearing something that primarily caters to our own comforts and desires. God speaks in order to accomplish *His* will, not ours.

We quiet our own voice by dying to self. As Christians, we take up our cross and follow Christ. As we daily sacrifice self-centeredness for the sake of our Lord who laid down His life for us, we will be able to hear the voice of God more clearly.

Other People's Voices

Rather than hearing God's voice, we may also hear other people's voices vying for our attention. These voices are not to be confused with those people who give us godly counsel. These are the voices we hear deep inside, which have been placed there by persons who try to sell us their products or philosophies. These are the subconscious voices we have collected over time—ideas and concepts we have been taught or experienced through living. Whenever these thoughts and opinions are hostile to the Word of God or distort the Word of God, we are told to demolish them (see 2 Cor. 10:5).

The truth is that our histories mold us, sometimes to our detriment. A middle-aged man told me that he felt he would never amount to anything because he had heard his father tell him so as a child. He had allowed this voice spoken years before to influence his life, rather than the voice of his heavenly Father who says, "I love you and I am pleased with you. I have a purpose for your life."

What we have been told about ourselves, and our world (what was reflected back to us even at a very early age), will become what we believe. If these beliefs are in disagreement with God's truth, they are misperceptions and distort our ability to hear from God clearly.

The Voice of the Enemy

A few years ago, a young man in his late teens stopped by our house and declared that he had heard God's voice. A strange expression came over his face, and then he spelled it out. "The Lord spoke to me today . . . and he told me to kill myself."

I was momentarily stunned! I obviously knew from the Word of God that the Lord would never tell someone to kill himself. It was clear that the young man was hearing another voice. This brings us to a third voice we may hear—the voice of the enemy.

Contrary to popular opinion, the devil does not appear to us in a red jumpsuit with a long tail and sprouting horns. He most often comes very slyly as an angel of light (see 2 Cor. 11:14). He may place thoughts into our mind that are contrary to God's Word, or use well-meaning people to speak words that could water down our faith. The devil often quotes Scripture and uses spiritual-sounding language.

His goal is to confuse, entrap and derail. He wants to get people to question God's character and turn them away from Him. He aims to confuse us and get us off track.

How often have you decided to get serious about studying the Scriptures and a voice reminds you that you are hungry, or that there is a TV program you really want to watch or chores that need to be completed immediately? Tell the devil the same thing that Jesus told him: "The scripture says, 'Human beings cannot live on bread alone, but need every word that God speaks'" (Matt. 4:4, *TEV*). "Submit yourselves, then, to God. Resist the devil, and he will flee from you" (Jas. 4:7-8).

God's Voice

As a Christian, the voice that you strive to hear and obey is the voice of God speaking to your spirit. He wants to speak to you!

Psalm 46:10 invites us to "be still, and know that I am God." It is so important to take time to be quiet and listen to the Lord speak. If we meet with a close friend and do all the talking without listening, the relationship is one-sided. In our prayers to the Lord, we should talk, but we must also learn to listen.

God is constantly speaking to us. We must tune in to the right frequency to hear Him. Radio, television and cell phone signals are all around us in the atmosphere, but we need the proper receiver to hear these signals or see the pictures projected to our TV set. In the same vein, we must place ourselves in a listening posture in order to hear God's voice.

Samuel, a young boy who later became a mighty prophet in the Bible, learned as a small boy to hear the Lord's voice; but it was a process (see 1 Sam. 3:1-12). He didn't even recognize it was the Lord when God first spoke to him.

In the beginning, the voice sounded like his mentor Eli. Perhaps God first spoke to Samuel in a voice that was familiar to him so that he would not be frightened. I believe that God often speaks through a voice that you will recognize. Sometimes it may sound like your own voice or even your own thoughts, while at other times, God may speak through someone you know. If it is God's voice, even if it is unclear at first, it will always lead to His peace inside you.

Just like Samuel, you have to learn to discern if you are hearing the Lord's voice or another voice. Don't worry if you feel like a modern-day Samuel who does not recognize God's voice right away; you will learn in time! Listening takes time and requires discernment.

Discernment Comes with Practice

The writer of Hebrews tells us that we can train ourselves to recognize the voice of God above all the various other voices. "Solid food is for mature people who have been trained to know right from wrong" (Heb. 5:14, *CEV*). It is through practice that we are able to discern whether what we hear is God's voice, our own voice, or the devil's.

A basketball player was asked how he scored the game-winning 3-pointer under incredible pressure and said, "That's why I've practiced 3-pointers every day for years." Through practice he trained his body to shoot in an almost automatic fashion. Just so, discernment comes with practice. You have to constantly evaluate your beliefs, feelings, other people's voices, the media and your own inner life in light of God's Word. Over time, you train your senses to do it almost by reflex.

Ask God to communicate to you during your prayer times with Him and all throughout the day. You will learn more and more to discern the difference between your voice, others' voices, the voice of the enemy and the voice of the Holy Spirit. You will learn how to hear the voice of God and obey Him. Remember, listening is an art.

Discerning of Spirits

The Lord also speaks to us through the supernatural gift of discerning of spirits. Some translations of the Bible call this gift "distinguishing between spirits" (1 Cor. 12:10). The gift of discerning of spirits is the supernatural power to detect the realm of the spirits and decipher their activities. It is the supernatural revelation whether something is or is not of God. Discerning of spirits is done by the power of the Holy Spirit who bears witness with our spirit.

Did you ever meet a person for the first time and sense there is something wrong? It may be the Lord manifesting the gift of discerning of spirits to you so that you can respond accordingly. Paul experienced this in events recorded in Acts 16, when a girl started following him, shouting that he was a servant of God. Paul discerned, however, that it was an evil spirit within her that was recognizing God's divine power in him. Paul discerned that the spirit in the girl was demonic and cast it out. The results of this girl being delivered from an evil spirit opened the door for the gospel to be preached in the city of Philippi.

Ask the Lord to make you discerning and also ask Him for a spiritual gift of discerning of spirits. It will save you lots of struggle in your future and open doors for great blessing as you hear His voice clearly.

Apply What You've Learned

VERSE TO REMEMBER:

We demolish arguments and every pretension that sets itself up against the knowledge of God, and we take captive every thought to make it obedient to Christ.
2 CORINTHIANS 10:5-6

1. Describe a time when you knew it was not God's voice but another voice you were hearing.

2. How have you ever confused your own desires with the voice of the Lord? How did you finally know it was happening?

3. How does discerning God's voice come with practice?

41

Resisting the Devil

I was driving down the road in my car one day when a spirit of fear came on me like a cloud. I was paralyzed with fear. Fortunately, I was aware of what was happening. The enemy wanted me to live by my feelings of fear rather than do the things I knew God was calling me to do. I said boldly, "In Jesus' name, I renounce this spirit of fear and command it to leave." And guess what? It left! When we resist the devil, he has to flee.

We do not have to put up with a spirit of fear or any other affliction that the devil will try to bring against us. Jesus Christ has come to set us free! James 4:7 says, "Submit yourselves, then, to God. Resist the devil, and he will flee from you."

Sometimes because of demonic activity, we cannot hear God speak to us. To be set free from demonic bondage you must resist the devil by prayer and proclaim God's Word as you call upon the mighty name of Jesus. It is fascinating to notice that after you are encouraged in James 4:7 to "resist the devil," the next verse immediately says that you should "come near to God and he will come near to you." If you cannot hear the voice of God because of demonic activity in your life, you must resist the devil and then without delay turn your attention to God. He will speak to you as He draws near to you.

Smith Wigglesworth was an evangelist in Great Britain years ago. He compared the devil to a stray dog barking at our heels. He taught that unless we resist the dog, he will continue with his "yelping" and aggravation. But if we boldly tell him to leave us alone, he will flee. The devil has no choice when we resist him in Jesus' name. He must flee.

As Christians, we can call upon Jesus to help us with spiritual battles. Matthew 12:29-30 says that we can tie up the strong man (Satan) and rob his house (set free those who are enslaved to Satan). "Or again, how can anyone enter a strong man's house and carry off his possessions unless he first ties up the strong man? Then he can rob his house" (Matt. 12:29-30).

We can drive demons out in the name of Jesus by "tying up" the demonic spirit that is influencing our life or someone else's life. Only then can we be free. As believers, we can provide deliverance for those who have been held captive by Satan's power. "And these signs will accompany those who believe: In my name they will drive out demons" (Mark 16:17).

Casting out demons is a ministry that the Lord has given to those who believe in Him. Christians are called to minister deliverance to those bound by Satan. If you believe the Lord is calling you to set people free from demonic spirits, I encourage you to follow the example of Jesus. Jesus sent His disciples out two by two to minister. They did not minister alone. And they came back excited! Why? "Even the demons submit to us in your name," they said (Luke 10:17).

We should note that Jesus gives His disciples a word of caution: "Do not rejoice that the spirits submit to you, but rejoice that your names are written in heaven" (Luke 10:20). Jesus cautioned the disciples to not make the power over the demons the source of their joy, but to rejoice because of their relationship with Him.

The fact remained—demons could not stand in the presence of the disciples who were commissioned by Jesus to cast them out. The Lord has also commissioned us to cast demons out of people and be set free from demonic activity in our own life in Jesus' powerful name!

Renounce Demonic Spirits

Sometimes people get involved innocently with the demonic by dabbling in paranormal energies in order to gain knowledge of the future or uncover secrets—reading tarot cards, playing demonic games like the Ouija board, water witching, having séances to contact the dead, using drugs to produce "spiritual experiences"—all these kinds of practices are associated with the occult. Attempting to communicate with the supernatural through these kinds of methods is actually communication with demons (see 1 Sam. 28:8-14; 2 Kings 21:6; Isa. 8:19).

Getting involved in these kinds of occult practices is dangerous and can lead to demonic bondage. The Bible gives these warnings: "Do not practice divination or sorcery" (Lev. 19:26). "Do not turn to mediums or seek out spiritists, for you will be defiled by them. I am the Lord your God" (Lev. 19:31).

As a young boy, I participated in a type of divination by trying to "smell for water" on our family farm. We believed that by holding a rod, we could locate underground streams of water, thus knowing where to drill a well. Although I was completely unaware of it at the time, I was dabbling in the occult. Trying to uncover the unknown forces of nature by using superstitious practices like this is really opening us to demonic spirits. After I received Jesus Christ as Lord, I claimed my freedom from the curse the enemy tried to place over my life through my involvement in this occult practice. Years ago, I also played with a Ouija board, a game that attempts to uncover secret things by submitting to unknown spiritual forces. Again, I broke that curse over my life in the name of Jesus Christ.

There are two supernatural powers—the power of God through Jesus Christ, and the power of the enemy. A curse can be placed over our life if we are involved in any type of occult practices. I have ministered to people who had an intense desire to commit suicide or who fell into depression because the devil held them in bondage due to their involvement in the occult. The good news is this: you can be set completely free! If you or your ancestors have been involved in any type of occult activity, you can be set free. When you renounce those demonic spirits in the name of Jesus, the demons can no longer have any control of your life.

A friend of ours had migraine headaches for more than eight years. In her case, this physical ailment was tied into her involvement in the occult. In desperation, she went to some Christians for help. They rebuked the devil in Jesus' name, and she was set free from the curse of constant headaches over her life.

Our lives are like an onion with many layers of skin. Maybe you have been set free from demonic spirits in your life. There may be little layers that God has already peeled off. However, the Lord may take you through other areas of freedom in the future.

He loves us and leads us step by step. He knows what we can handle. As the Lord reveals other areas of bondage in our life, we receive His freedom. Then another layer comes off. The Lord continues this process until we are completely clean and are the people God has called us to be. He is committed to seeing us set completely free so that we can hear His voice clearly.[1] This process may take days, months or even years.

Our Spiritual Weapons

As Christians, we are engaged in a spiritual conflict with evil. Although we have been guaranteed victory through Christ's death on the cross, we must wage a spiritual warfare by the power of the Holy Spirit, using our spiritual armor (see Eph. 6:10-18). The first weapon is the "name of Jesus

Christ." The Scriptures tell us, "That at the name of Jesus every knee should bow, in heaven and on earth and under the earth, and every tongue confess that Jesus Christ is Lord, to the glory of God the Father" (Phil. 2:10-11).

Some time ago, I was awakened in the night and sensed an evil presence in my room. I was away from home, and no one else was in the house where I was staying. I felt like I was frozen to my bed. I could only call out the name of Jesus. The evil presence left and I was able to go back to sleep. There is power in the name of Jesus.

The second weapon the Lord has given to us is the "blood of Jesus Christ." I have actually witnessed demons in people who have shrieked in fear at the mention of the blood of Jesus. On one occasion, a man with demons held his hands over his ears and screamed when the blood of Jesus was mentioned. The blood of the Lamb has freed us from the power of the enemy. The Scriptures tell us in Revelation 12:11, "They overcame him by the blood of the Lamb and by the word of their testimony; they did not love their lives so much as to shrink from death."

The third weapon the Lord has given us against the curse of the enemy is the "word of our testimony." Our testimony is simply confessing what the Lord has done in our life and what God is saying about us by believing the truth of His Word. The truth of God's Word sets us free from the noise of life so that we can hear His voice clearly.

Apply What You've Learned

VERSE TO REMEMBER:

Submit yourselves, then, to God. Resist the devil, and he will flee from you.

JAMES 4:7

1. Why should we resist the devil and then turn our attention to God?

2. How can we renounce demonic spirits?

3. Explain how our spiritual weapons help us fight spiritual battles (see Eph. 6:10-18).

Note

1. For more about being set free, see Larry Kreider's book *Freedom from the Curse* (Lititz, PA: House to House Publications, 2002).

42

Silencing Voices from the Past

A famous zoo in Germany purchased a great brown bear from the traveling circus. Until this point, this magnificent but abused creature had lived in misery. For the duration of its life the bear had been locked up in a tiny circus cage about 12 feet long. Every waking hour of the day, with its massive head swaying back and forth in rhythm, he took 12 steps forward and 12 steps backward in his narrow prison. The water given to him was stagnant; the food was rotten.

Finally he was sold and transferred from his tiny cage to the beautiful German zoo. The zoo had a bear compound consisting of acres of lush green grass. There were trees to climb and sparkling pools of fresh drinking water. The bear would be fed three meals each day and have other bear companions.

The zookeepers wheeled the bear's cage into the compound of the zoo and opened the door to freedom. The bear continued his march—12 feet forward and 12 feet back. They called out to him, but he would not respond. They offered him food. They offered him freedom, but he still would not respond.

Finally, the only solution left was to put some rags on a stick, soak them in kerosene, light them and place the burning rags through the bars. This scared the bear enough to leave the cage. The bear looked around, and to the zoo attendant's amazement, he started pacing 12 feet forward and 12 feet back—the exact dimensions of his cage!

Suddenly it dawned on the attendants—the bear's prison was not a metal one, but an invisible mental one! They could do nothing to help him out of his prison and finally had to put him to sleep.

Some Christians find themselves in a similar dilemma. Having become so accustomed to certain thought patterns of defeat and failure in some areas of their life, they convince themselves that things will never change and they remained locked in an invisible mental prison. Precious, born-again, Spirit-filled Christians who love Jesus with all their heart are susceptible to this kind of mental trap. Some, upon facing incredible obstacles in life, become weary and settle for far less than the Lord intended for them. God wants us to silence those voices of defeat so that we can hear from Him.

Set Free!

When we join God's family, we are set free from the power of sin over our life; we are set free from its guilt. Jesus tells us in John 8:31-32, "If you hold to my teaching, you are really my disciples. Then you will know the truth, and the truth will set you free."

The first part of that verse says that we must continue in God's Word—love it, keep it and walk in it—and we shall know the truth and experience freedom. No one is truly free until the power of sin has been rendered inoperative as we consider ourselves dead to sin and alive to God. The Bible tells us that we are adopted into God's family. "For you did not receive a spirit that makes you a slave again to fear, but you received the Spirit of sonship. And by him we cry, 'Abba, Father'" (Rom. 8:15).

Every person living in sin is subject to fear because he is guilty! His conscience will trouble him. But a Christian does not have this fear because he has been adopted as a child into God's family (see John 1:12, Eph. 1:5, Gal. 4:5).

The Devil Condemns; God Convicts

When we sin, the devil will tell us that it is a long way back to God. He will try to make us believe that God will never use us again. But we now know better. If we sin, we must repent (stop sinning and change direction). The Lord forgives us, and we start with a clean slate.

At times, restitution has to follow repentance. Restitution involves putting things right with people we have wronged. If someone repents from shoplifting, he needs to pay back what he stole. Although he is forgiven the moment he confesses his sin, he needs to take a step of obedience and restore what was stolen. When Zacchaeus repented for running a crooked tax collection agency, he told the Lord he would restore four times what he had stolen (see Luke 19:8-9).

The devil condemns us, but God convicts us of our sin. Don't accept condemnation from Satan or from other people. "Therefore, there is now no condemnation for those who are in Christ Jesus, because through Christ Jesus the law of the Spirit of life set me free from the law of sin and death" (Rom. 8:1-2).

Jesus Christ has made you free! You are free from the law of sin and death. He has made you righteous by faith in Him.

Expect to Hear from God!

The psalmist directed his prayers to God expecting an answer, "In the morning I lay my requests before you and wait in expectation" (Ps. 5:3). God wants us to make our first petitions to Him each day as we live in expectancy of an answer. Jeremiah 33:3 says, "Call unto me and I will answer you and show you great and mighty things." When we seek God, He promises to answer—of that we can be sure.

Loren Cunningham, founder of Youth With A Mission (YWAM), says that he has found three simple steps that have helped him and thousands of others to hear God's voice:

1. *Submit to His Lordship.* Ask Him to help you silence your thoughts, desires and the opinions of others that may be filling your mind (see 2 Cor. 10:5). Although you have been given a good mind to use, you want to hear the thoughts of the Lord, who has the best mind (see Prov. 3:5-6).

2. *Resist the enemy* in case he is trying to deceive you. Use the authority that Jesus Christ has given you to silence the voice of the enemy (see Jas. 4:7; Eph. 6:10-20).

3. *Expect an answer.* After asking the question that is on your mind, wait for Him to answer. Expect your loving heavenly Father to speak to you, and He will (see John 10:27; Ps. 69:13; Exod. 33:11).

Hearing from God is a journey. After many years of listening for His voice, I still sometimes make mistakes in hearing clearly. But I am learning, and you will too! Just as a young baby quickly learns to know his daddy's voice and responds to it by turning toward that loving, familiar voice, you will learn to hear God's voice as you love Him and obey Him.

Apply What You've Learned

VERSE TO REMEMBER:

Therefore, there is now no condemnation for those who are in Christ Jesus,
because through Christ Jesus the law of the Spirit of life set me free from
the law of sin and death.

ROMANS 8:1-2

1. How do patterns of failure in areas of your life convince you that you cannot change?

2. Who is the author of condemnation? Of conviction?

3. Describe some areas in which Christ has set you free so that you can hear from Him.

43

Finding Freedom

A young man and his fiancée came to me for premarital counseling. The young man had experienced many hurts in his life. For one, his father had constantly blamed him for the problems in his marriage because the son was conceived out of wedlock. The young man was hurting and in need of healing. I asked him if he was willing to forgive his dad. He was willing. We laid hands on him and prayed for him to be healed of the painful memories he received while growing up.

The young man had a wonderful wedding a few months later. His father was at the wedding and there was no longer a wall between them. God had healed the young man. The pain was gone. God supernaturally healed him because Jesus Christ took that pain on the cross 2,000 years ago.

Many Christians long for a deeper, closer relationship with the Lord, but they have a hard time hearing from God as they continue to struggle with the same fears and hurtful memories from their past, unable to break free. Crippled emotionally, they need to be set free from the curse of painful memories and hurts. It is not God's will for people's hearts to be broken. He wants to heal us emotionally, according to Luke 4:18-19: "The Spirit of the Lord is on me, because he has anointed me to preach good news to the poor. He has sent me to proclaim freedom for the prisoners and recovery of sight for the blind, to release the oppressed, to proclaim the year of the Lord's favor."

The term "inner healing" is used for explaining emotional healing. To receive inner healing means to be healed of lie-filled memories or to have our broken hearts healed. Sometimes our present emotional pain comes from the misinterpretation (lies) embedded in our memories and not from the memories themselves. For example, an incest victim feels shame not because she was molested but because she may believe it was her fault (lie). When the lie is exposed, she can receive freedom.

Inner healing, or the healing of memories, is a very valid ministry in the Body of Christ today. If we believe that someone has hurt us and continue to remember those hurts and the memories of what happened, we need to be healed emotionally. We can be made whole. Jesus wants to heal us and set us free. The healing of memories does not mean that we no longer remember what has happened. We may remember what happened, but the pain is healed through Jesus revealing the truth to us. Eventually, we can look back and give praise to God for His healing on our life and His grace and strength to go on.

The healing process is often just that, a process. It can, but often does not, happen overnight. One of the keys to being set free is to forgive.

Forgive, Forgive, Forgive

An important scriptural principle to being healed and set free is found in Matthew 6:14-15: "For if you forgive men when they sin against you, your heavenly Father will also forgive you. But if you do not forgive men their sins, your Father will not forgive your sins."

This is important! We must forgive those who have hurt us in order for God to heal us. In Matthew 18, Jesus tells a parable about a servant who owed his king $1 million. He begged the king for extra time to pay the debt, and the king took pity on him and canceled the whole debt. The servant then went out and found one of his fellow servants who owed him $2,000. He grabbed him by the shirt and demanded immediate payment. The fellow servant pleaded for more time, but the servant refused and had the debtor thrown into prison. The king discovered what had happened and called the servant in. "I forgave you $1 million and you couldn't forgive someone a few thousand dollars? I showed you mercy but you could not show mercy to another?" Then the Scriptures make an interesting statement, "In anger his master turned him over to the jailers to be tortured, until he should pay back all he owed. This is how my heavenly Father will treat each of you unless you forgive your brother from your heart" (Matt. 18:34-35).

The king had the man thrown into prison for not showing forgiveness to another. Jesus says that if we don't forgive someone who has hurt us or ripped us off, God will deliver us to the torturers or demons of hell. Even Christians at times can be tormented with confusion, frustration, depression or other ills brought on by the demons of hell if they choose not to forgive. Unforgiveness leaves the door wide open for the devil!

Forgiving those who have hurt us is the first step to being set free. We may not feel like it, but because God forgave us, we need to forgive others. God will bring emotional healing as we obey His Word and forgive from our heart in faith.

And Forgive Some More!

In addition to forgiving the person who has hurt us, we must also ask God to forgive the person. Asking God to forgive him or her is a vital second step of forgiveness we need to take so that we can be set free. Stephen, when he was being stoned, said, "Lord, do not hold this sin against them" (Acts 7:60). Jesus, on the cross, said, "Father, forgive them, for they do not know what they are doing" (Luke 23:34).

A third step is to ask God to forgive us for any wrong attitudes or any attempt to hide our sin. Proverbs 28:13 says, "He who conceals his sins does not prosper, but whoever confesses and renounces them finds mercy." The word "prosper" means "to break out of bondage." If we hide our sin and are not honest about it, we cannot break out of the bondage of the sin. If we don't ask God to heal us for wrong attitudes, then we cannot prosper in this area of our life.

A fourth step is to confess our faults to someone and have him or her pray for us so that God will heal us. The Scripture says in James 5:16, "Therefore confess your sins to each other and pray for each other so that you may be healed. The prayer of a righteous man is powerful and effective."

Ask someone to lay hands on you and pray for your emotional healing. This is why it is so important to be connected to the rest of the Body of Christ through a local church. As you meet together with other believers, ask the Lord to show you someone you can trust to pray for you. The Lord wants to heal you and set you free.

A Sound Mind

We live in a day of extreme stress. Many of us face mental anguish. Jesus came to set us free from this curse on our mind that has its root based in unwholesome fear. The Scriptures tell us in 2 Timothy 1:7, "For God has not given us a spirit of fear, but of power and of love and of a sound mind" (NKJV).

God's purpose for your life is for you to have a sound mind. Perhaps your ancestors had some type of mental problems. God says that you can be free from that curse in Jesus' name. As I was growing up, I can vividly remember various members of my extended family who had a history of mental illness. I feared that I would spend periods of my life in a mental hospital like some of my family members. One day I came to the realization that I didn't have to fear mental illness because Jesus Christ became a curse for me. By the grace of God, I have been freed from that curse.

The Lord's will for each of us is to have peace of mind. The Bible says that the Lord "will keep in perfect peace him whose mind is steadfast, because he trusts in you" (Isa. 26:3).

Since I have been set free from the curse, in Jesus' name, the Lord has delivered me from the fear of mental illness. We serve a good God. We can trust Him. He has promised us perfect peace as we continue to focus on our heavenly Father, the author of all peace (see 1 Cor. 14:33). You and I are in a brand-new family, the family of God, through faith in Jesus Christ. We have a brand-new household, the household of God. Our new Father in heaven does not have any mental problems at all.

We can break every curse that is over our life, in Jesus' name. By the grace of God, I have broken every curse over my life. I am a free man! Today is your day of freedom. Today is the day for any curse over your life to be completely broken. God has created you to commune with Him. When we are free from the noise of demonic bondages, we are then in a position to hear God's voice clearly.

Apply What You've Learned

VERSE TO REMEMBER:

The Spirit of the Lord is on me . . . to release the oppressed.
LUKE 4:18

1. What is inner healing?

2. Why is forgiveness so important to your healing and freedom?

3. How does breaking every curse over your life put you in a position to better hear God?

DIVINE ENCOUNTERS

44

A Daily Encounter

Daily time set aside to meet with God should be like a visit with your closest friend. We make time for close friends and look forward to their visits. The Lord cherishes time with us too. He is a God of relationship. He created us with a desire to have close and intimate relationships. First and foremost, we were created to have a relationship with Him and then with one another.

Why is it so vitally important for every believer to have a daily time alone with God? Although we may "pray without ceasing" and walk with the Lord minute by minute, designating a special time of day to be alone with the Lord is vital to relating heart to heart with God. It helps to give a divine rhythm to our daily routine as we place ourselves in a position to hear from God.

I have a great relationship with my wife, and we often communicate by cell phone or in personal contact many times throughout the day; however, LaVerne still appreciates a special night when we can spend time alone together without distractions. We call it our "date night" and keep that regular appointment even though we have been married for more than three decades. That time together is important in our relationship.

Making time with God a daily priority is saying that our relationship with the Lord is important and therefore we will set apart concentrated time to build this relationship. Yet, so frequently, we find it hard to commit to a daily time with God. We fall into a rut of allowing our time with God to become a drudgery or an obligation.

Max Lucado writes that because some of us have tried to have daily time with God and not been successful, we practice a type of surrogate spirituality in which we rely on others to spend time with God and try to benefit from their experience.

> Isn't that why we pay preachers . . . read Christian books? These folks are good at daily devotions. I'll just learn from them. If your spiritual experiences are secondhand . . . I'd like

to challenge you. . . . You don't say, "Vacations are such a hassle . . . I'm going to send someone on vacation for me." No! You want the experience firsthand.[1]

The simple fact remains—if we truly want an intimate, grace-filled relationship with God, we have to spend time alone with Him on a regular basis. Listening to God is a firsthand experience.

Listening Room

Ralph Neighbour suggests that our meeting time with God should involve much more than a one-way conversation in which we speak to God. He says, "It also involves listening to him, and [we all] need a listening room where we can hear the directions of God for our own needs, the needs of others and for his assignments to us."[2]

A Japanese pastor invited an American pastor to visit his home. The Japanese pastor took his guest to a lovely garden behind the house, where a one-room cottage stood. The pastor explained, "This is my 'listening room.' " Our "listening room" is more an attitude, a value of our lives, than a special room built for that purpose. It is a condition in which we not only speak to Him, but also hear from Him. God does speak![3]

When we spend time listening for God to speak, He will! Our daily encounters with God place us in a position to seek Him on behalf of not only our own needs but the needs of others as well. We are part of the Body of Christ, and our priestly task is to pray and intercede for others. Ralph says that "in these daily 'listenings' we become the priest of God, bringing the body members before him and coming away with edification for our fellow members."[4] Our alone time with God gives us the opportunity to hear Him speak so that we can be encouraged and in turn can encourage others.

What Works for You?

Avoiding legalistic approaches to spending time with the Lord will help you keep the time fresh and inviting. First of all, never allow others' expectations to manipulate your emotions and make you feel guilty for not devoting an hour or two alone with God each day. Although some people will easily spend an hour or more each day with God, others may have to start at 5, 10 or 15 minutes, and increase it over time. Allow the peace of God to rule in your heart about the time you believe God wants you to spend with Him. The best length of time spent with God is the time you will actually practice! Start with a realistic goal.

If you want your encounters to stay fresh, you cannot do it out of legalism but instead, because you hear God calling you each day, saying, "Arise, my love . . . and come away" (Song of Sol. 2:10). If you miss a day or two, God is not disappointed in you. He always welcomes you back with open arms. He is thrilled when you seek a friendship with Him.

You should pick the time of day that works for you. It works best for me to spend time alone with the Lord in the morning. I find that I am most alert and can give God my peak concentration in the morning; but everyone is different. So find the time, readjust your priorities and plan for it.

Two main activities of spending time with God are reading the Bible and prayer. The Bible is God speaking to humanity. Reading the Bible opens the door to communication from God. I use a Bible reading plan that takes me through the Bible at my own pace.[5]

For much of my life, I have found spending time alone with God each day in prayer to be hard work. I really wanted to be a man of prayer, but there was something desperately missing in my prayer life. I had seasons of victory in personal prayer but found myself often failing miserably. Then I had an experience that changed my life. Seven years ago, while in Uzbekistan, ministering to leaders of the underground Church, the Lord deeply convicted me about my lack of daily prayer through the lives of the praying believers I met. I came home desperate to learn to pray.

Like so many others I meet who are really honest, I wanted to be a man of prayer, but I needed to learn how to pray. During the next few years, I studied how Jesus taught His disciples to pray, and I discovered that He used the Lord's Prayer to teach them (see Luke 11). Hidden within the Lord's Prayer, I found 12 types of prayer to help me pray. My prayer life was transformed. It went from duty to joy. I now find fulfillment and joy in daily prayer (see Isa. 56:7). I explain how I have found daily prayer to be a great joy in my book *Building Your Personal House of Prayer.*[6]

A Two-Way Conversation

Prayer is simply a two-way conversation between you and God. When you spend time alone with a friend, you start to understand your friend's hopes, dreams and wants. You do this by speaking and by taking time to listen to your friend. Communication is incomplete if all you do is talk.

The more listening time you spend with your heavenly Father, the better you will understand His heart for you. Do not expect God to function simply as a drive-thru fast-food restaurant. While we may place our order (heart's desire), we must take time to hear His heart's desire on the matter. God always knows what is best and always has the timing exact.

God seeks to quiet the noise in order to make way for His voice to be heard. When is the last time you got away for an extended period of time without technology at your fingertips, where you just sat and quieted yourself on the beach or in another natural setting, or simply closed the door and sat in silence waiting on God?

To hear God's voice, we must find ways to be quiet and listen for the Lord to speak. God desires our closeness. He wants our unwavering love. Developing a love relationship with the Lord changes us in the depth of our being. Let God have all of you as you develop a listening heart that is open to hear His whispers.

Apply What You've Learned

VERSE TO REMEMBER:

Blessed is the man who listens to me, watching daily at my doors.
PROVERBS 8:34

1. Do you have a listening room? What do you do there?
2. How do you keep your time with God each day from becoming an obligation?
3. Discuss the ways God speaks to you in your daily encounter with Him.

Notes
1. Max Lucado, *Just Like Jesus* (Nashville, TN: Word Publishing, 1998), p. 45.
2. Ralph W. Neighbour, Jr., *The Arrival Kit* (Houston, TX: Touch Publications, 1993), p. 62.
3. Ibid., pp. 60-61.
4. Ibid., p. 69.
5. You can access this "Bible reading plan" by visiting our ministry's website at www.dcfi.org.
6. Larry Kreider, *Building Your Personal House of Prayer* (Shippensburg, PA: Destiny Image Publishers, Inc., 2008).

45

God's Character

After more than 36 years in a loving marriage, I know the character of my wife, LaVerne. I am confident that she would not intentionally speak harmful words or make rash decisions that would hurt me or betray me. All of her actions, including words of correction, are for my own good because she loves me. I trust her. I trust her character.

Many people don't really know God's character. Some think of Him as a distant disciplinarian who is just waiting to strike them for doing something wrong. Others think of God as a cosmic Santa Claus who gives everybody what they want and is there to make their lives pleasant and secure. We probably all have some distortions in our mind regarding the character of God, depending on our life experiences.

As we saturate ourselves in God's written revelation, the Bible, we get a clear picture of a God who is both loving and just, and who is faithful and consistent. As we understand His character, we listen with a trusting ear and can quickly tell if what we are hearing is consistent with who we know God to be.

How we see the character of God affects our relationship with him. Since God will never tell us to do anything that opposes His character, we must get to know the very nature of God so that we can be sure we are hearing from Him. We must understand His compassionate nature and how He longs for our intimacy and trust.

One of the most familiar verses in the Bible states, "For God so loved the world" (John 3:16). God's nature is revealed in this revelation of God as the Lover of mankind. God is love, and He loves us (see 1 John 4:7-8). We are precious in His sight, and He yearns for us. He wants to reveal Himself to us. He is passionately pursuing us!

The familiar Scripture verse goes on to say that God so loved the world that "He gave." He not only wants us to be lovers of people as He is, but He also wants us to be givers. He wants us to act like He does—and that is possible because His Word tells us that we are daily being conformed to the likeness of Christ (see Rom. 8:29). For example, He always tells the truth. He sets the example for us to do the same and be truthful with people—be true to our word.

The Bible tells us that God "made known His ways to Moses, His acts to the children of Israel" (Ps. 103:7, *NKJV*). Because Moses was in relationship with the Lord, he had learned to know the character of the Lord; however, the children of Israel only saw the things that God *did,* because they did not have a personal relationship with Him. When we get to know God and develop a love relationship with Him, we will know what God wants us to do. He will "make known" His ways to us.

God Reveals Himself Through His Love

First Corinthians 13:4-8 offers us a description of what love is. When we substitute the word "God" for the word "love" in these verses, we get an accurate picture of God's character. "God is patient, God is kind. God does not envy, God does not boast, God is not proud. God is not rude, God is not self-seeking, God is not easily angered, God keeps no record of wrongs. God does not delight in evil but rejoices with the truth. God always protects, always trusts, always hopes, always perseveres. God never fails."

God's love is revealed so that mankind can be liberated. The Scriptures tell us the Lord is one "who forgives all your iniquities, who heals all your diseases, who redeems your life from destruction, who crowns you with lovingkindness and tender mercies" (Ps. 103:3-4, *NKJV*). This is who our God is! He is a God who is forgiving. Our God heals us and redeems our life from destruction.

God's Character Shines Through

Sometimes we feel that we cannot hear from God because we are not righteous enough. But the truth is that Jesus has made us righteous by faith in Him. When God looks at us He sees Jesus first! No matter where you are in your spiritual journey with Christ, God sees the beauty of Jesus in you.

When we know Jesus' character, we can also sense if He is speaking through someone who claims to speak for God. Several years ago, when I pastored a church, a visiting speaker gave a specific "word" for me and my leadership team. Our team considered his "word" but did not feel that we should do what he was suggesting. The very next day, he called me and gave another "word," even using Scripture to pronounce it. Our team met together and united in prayer to receive the Lord's protection because we sensed this action was spiritual manipulation on the part of the speaker. We learned later that this man had brought division and strife to many churches through his "words from God" for them. We knew that what the speaker had said was not a word from God, because it was not compatible with the character of Christ.

God's Character Reveals His Heart

Christ wants to give us a full, abundant life, and He's told us so: "I have come that they may have life, and have it to the full" (John 10:10).

The word "life" is a translation of the Greek word *zoe*, which, when used in Scripture, implies "the very nature of God and source of life." The abundant life then, is life filled with the very nature of God inside of us. This life is abundant in quantity and quality—overflowing life. That is the kind of life that God has prepared for us as His children.

As we learn to walk and talk with God over a period of years, we get to know His heart, His character, His ways. If we are committed to following His character and His ways, He can give us a greater liberty because we become "one with Him." As our spirit becomes filled with His Spirit, and our desires begin to merge with His, we walk in His ways. Jesus said, "I and the Father are one" (John 10:30) and "I do nothing on my own but speak just what the Father has taught me" (John 8:28). Jesus was one with His Father and was given freedom by His Father on Earth. He knew His heavenly Father so well that He modeled His Father's character and only did what He saw His Father doing.

The Bible says, "Delight yourself in the LORD and he will give you the desires of your heart" (Ps. 37:4; see also Ps. 20:4). This means that He puts His desires into our hearts as we follow Him. A friend of mine was involved in politics for many years, but the Lord took the desire away and gave him a heart for mentoring younger leaders. The Lord spoke to him by changing the desires of his heart.

Let's hear God speak to us by what He reveals through His character that extends to each of us His unconditional love, acceptance, forgiveness and righteousness.

Apply What You've Learned

VERSES TO REMEMBER:

If we confess our sins, he is faithful and just and will forgive us our sins and purify us from all unrighteousness.
1 JOHN 1:9

Whoever does not love does not know God, because God is love.
1 JOHN 4:8

1. How does God reveal His character?
2. How has God revealed Himself to you through His love?
3. How does God make His ways known to us through His character?

46

Angels

On a short-term mission trip to a Kenyan orphanage, Sharon was awakened by the sound of barking dogs. She glanced out the window and was awestruck to see a tall "being" clothed in a long, flowing white garment and floating about five feet from the ground as if standing watch on the dirt road that bordered the orphanage compound. She started praying and heard the Lord speak these words to her spirit: "I have sent my angel to guard and watch over this place." The next morning, she shared her sighting with the children. These refugee children had not been in safe places until they came to the orphanage, and their reaction was one of delight, along with a feeling of well-being and security.

God can and will speak to us in every way that He has spoken in the past, including speaking through angels, although such supernatural occurrences are not as common as other ways of hearing God.

Today's culture is fascinated with the topic of angels because it is searching for supernatural experience and spiritual meaning. We have TV shows, magazine articles and books taking the topic of angels quite seriously, but most reveal a very poor grasp of what the Bible teaches about angels. This only adds to the confusion of who holy angels really are and what they do.

Angels Are Messengers of God

The Bible tells us that God sends angels to deliver messages to His people. When angels speak or appear, we should listen to what they say. Angels are servants of God and are described as spirits "to help and care for those who are to receive his salvation" (Heb. 1:14, *TLB*). They are God's messengers to protect, provide, proclaim God's truth or carry out God's judgments. They are spiritual beings created by God to serve Him and man.

There are many, many incidences of angels appearing in the Bible. In both the Old and the New Testaments, angels were commonplace. They often delivered their message and quickly moved on. They rarely drew attention or glory to themselves. Their job was to work on the sidelines, mostly invisibly.

Many times angels appeared to guide, comfort and provide for God's people as they performed certain tasks. Sometimes they intervened in the affairs of nations or helped people in times of suffering or persecution.

An angel shut the lions' mouths when Daniel was thrown into their den. An angel appeared to Mary, telling her she would bear a son. An angel rolled away the stone from Jesus' tomb. Cornelius was visited by an angel who told him to send for Peter, and as a result, Peter was instrumental in leading Cornelius and his whole household to Christ.

Fallen Angels Do Not Speak for God

Although holy angels are the messengers of God, the Bible tells us there are also other angels—demons of darkness. God's holy angels remain obedient to God and carry out His will, but the fallen angels fell from their holy position and now try everything to thwart God's purposes here on Earth. God's holy angels war against the fallen angels on our behalf. The devil, we are told in the Bible, masquerades as an angel of light (see 2 Cor. 11:14). This is why we need to know the Word of God, so we can discern between the real and the counterfeit.

Regardless of our culture's fascination with angels, we should never contact angels, pray to them or worship them. In addition to not contradicting the Bible, any action of holy angels will glorify God and be consistent with His character.

How Angels Help, Comfort and Protect Us

If you are a Christian, according to the Bible you have angels looking out for you. God created angels to help accomplish His work in this world, and they watch over Christians and will assist us because we belong to God. Psalm 91:11 says, "For he will command his angels concerning you to guard you in all your ways."

When Peter was released from prison by an angel and arrived at the door of Mary's house, the believers meeting there could not believe it was Peter in person but said, "It must be his [guardian] angel" (Acts 12:7-15), which shows us the expectation of the Early Church to see angels. Jesus had told His followers earlier that those with childlike faith would have the services of angels, "their angels have constant access to my Father" (Matt. 18:10, *TLB*). As a believer, God provides angels for you because He loves you and will speak comfort and protection to you through these messengers.

You may not be aware of the presence of angels around you, and you cannot predict how they will appear. This explains the verse in the Bible that says, "Do not forget to entertain strangers, for by so doing some people have entertained angels without knowing it" (Heb. 13:2). Just because you have never seen an angel does not mean angels are not present with you. My wife is convinced that I have many angels who protect me while I drive, because I often get so preoccupied while driving that I need supernatural intervention to keep the car on the road!

Although angels are spirits, they make themselves visible when needed. There have been angelic sightings all over the world. I have a close relative who saw an angel in her bedroom to bring her comfort and hope during a time of great need. She told me a deep peace came over her when she had the angelic visitation.

Several years ago, a friend of mine was detained in Albania for handing out Bibles. Miraculously, she and her friend were released. The only problem was that they were out in the middle of nowhere, each with a heavy suitcase. It was miles to the Yugoslavian border. Miraculously, a man stopped and offered to drive them through the countryside and straight to the border. He dropped them off and was gone, returning the way he had come. They were convinced it was an angel who had provided help in their time of need.

John G. Paton, pioneer missionary in the New Hebrides Islands, told a thrilling story involving the protective care of angels. Hostile natives surrounded his mission headquarters one night, intent on burning the Patons out and killing them. The Patons prayed all during the terror-filled night that God would deliver them. When daylight came they were amazed to see that, unaccountably, the attackers had left. They thanked God for delivering them.

A year later, the chief of the tribe was converted to Jesus Christ, and Mr. Paton, remembering what had happened, asked the chief what had kept him and his men from burning down the house and killing them. The chief replied in surprise, "Who were all those men you had with you there?" The missionary answered, "There were no men there; just my wife and I." The chief argued that they had seen many men standing guard—hundreds of big men in shining garments with drawn swords in their hands. They seemed to circle the mission station so that the natives were afraid to attack. Only then did Mr. Paton realize that God had sent His angels to protect them.[1]

Even if we never see an angel physically, we should be aware of how close God's ministering angels are and sense their presence so that we can face each day, trusting God to care for us. Moreover, be sure to be kind to strangers; they could be angels sent from God to speak to you!

Apply What You've Learned

VERSE TO REMEMBER:

Are not all angels ministering spirits sent to serve those who will inherit salvation?
HEBREWS 1:14

1. Explain how angels are God's messengers.

2. What is their purpose for appearing to humans?

3. Have you or anyone you know ever had an encounter with an angel giving a message from God?

Note
1. Billy Graham, *Angels* (Dallas, TX: Word Publishing, 1986), p. 3.

47

His Silence

There are times when it seems the Lord is nowhere to be found. Our prayers feel like they are hitting the ceiling and bouncing back. We feel far from God—like we have entirely lost our way. Every Christian goes through these "dark nights of the soul" when the Lord seems to be silent.

You are not alone. Jesus understands how you feel. He cried out in anguish, "Father, why have You forsaken me?" Even Jesus knew His Father's silence.

Sometimes we fail to hear from God because we are not paying attention; but what about those times when we really are listening but somehow we can no longer sense Him speaking? At times, God's reasons for being silent are to get our attention so that we can receive clear spiritual direction that will go to the core of our being. His silence may occur when He is poised to do His deepest work in our life.

Realize How You Need God

We should not fear God's silence, because it really is a reminder that we need Him so desperately. When He is silent and life seems dark, it often motivates us to place our full trust in Him. We pay more attention when we are lost in the woods! God may be building our character so that we can be more effective in His kingdom. In the darkness of God's silence, we are reminded of what we are missing.

I was in a small group of leaders where Bob Mumford once said, "I do not trust anyone unless he walks with a limp." I agree with him. He was referring to Jacob, who, during a time of great trial in his life, wrestled with God, demanding His blessing. He was touched in his thigh and did in fact receive the Lord's blessing. But from that day on, he walked with a limp (see Gen. 32:22-32). When God lovingly deals with us in the difficult times, we walk with a spiritual limp the rest of our lives. This is the stuff of which true spiritual men and women of God are made.

Refuse to Quit

The Bible is filled with examples of those who started with an exciting experience of hearing from the Lord, refused to quit when God was silent and consequently experienced great fruitfulness because they kept their confidence and trust in the Lord. The story of Joseph in the Old Testament is one of the best examples.

After having a dream that his brothers would bow down to him, he encountered trial after trial. He was sold as a slave by his brothers, lied about by his employer's wife, imprisoned while innocent, forgotten in prison . . . only to become second in command of all Egypt, overnight! Although it must have felt to him that God had left him in prison to die, he entered a stage of great fruitfulness as he refused to give up during the difficult seasons of his life.

God used this stage of testing in Joseph's life to examine his character. God gave him an attitude check, and Joseph passed the test. He could then be a blessing to his brothers who had severely mistreated him in the past.

Many people quit during a testing period, when the Lord seems to stop speaking, and never experience the stage of fruitfulness the Lord has planned for them.

The Lord is much more concerned about what He is doing in you than about you reaching your goals. He wants you to depend on Him and on His power in the here and now. Oswald Chambers once said, "If I can stay calm, faithful, and unconfused while in the middle of the turmoil of life, the goal of the purpose of God is being accomplished in me. God is not working toward a particular finish—His purpose is the process itself."[1] God's silence will reveal our true attitudes toward Him by showing us what is really in our hearts and then giving us the opportunity to fully trust in His power as we persevere.

Examine Your Heart

It is true that God is sometimes silent due to no fault of our own, but because He is simply developing within us a depth of character and a deeper trust in Him; at other times, He is silent due to our disobedience. King David once said, "If I had not confessed the sin in my heart, my Lord would not have listened" (Ps. 66:18, *NLT*). Sin alienates us from God and creates a barrier to hearing from Him. In times like these, God's silences may be an act of judgment.

If we cannot hear God's voice because He is chastising us with His silence, we must examine ourselves to see what is hindering us from hearing. A few years ago, LaVerne and I bought a time-share near Orlando, Florida. Although there is nothing wrong with purchasing a time-share, we knew immediately that we had made a mistake. Instead of following our personal policy of taking time to pray and not make a quick decision, we bought it impulsively and under pressure from the sales pitch. We went off-track from what we knew was the Lord's best for us.

We quickly repented for not following our personal value of waiting and praying, and after asking the Lord to restore our mistake, I felt that He said He would redeem it for us in two years. And that is exactly what happened. Two years later we were able to sell it.

In Times of Suffering

God does not cause or permit tragedies to punish us. Sin is the cause of man's suffering. In this fallen, sinful world, we will have suffering; we can't avoid it. Jesus Himself suffered on the cross. Psalm 34:19 tells us that the good man does not escape all troubles—he has them too. God doesn't cause pain to teach us a lesson, but we definitely will learn from pain. Our response to God during times of grief and suffering can bring us closer to Him or take us further away. How do we respond to unanswered prayers? Or how do we respond when we pray and it seems like the opposite happens?

Prayers of Lament

"If what we asked God for doesn't happen, we are in good company," says Ron Parrish, in his book *From Duty to Delight*:

> Jesus' prayer to be delivered from the ordeal of the cross was denied. Before that He expressed a deep longing for the people of Jerusalem to accept Him and His message. It didn't happen. What are we to do with the disappointment of unanswered prayer? We must learn to lament in the presence of

the Father. David was an expert "lamenter." . . . Jesus quoted this prayer of lament of David: "My God, my God, why have you forsaken me? Why are you so far from saving me, so far from the words of my groaning? O my God, I cry out by day, but you do not answer, by night, and am not silent." Here's how it works: We bring before God the longings of our heart. If nothing seems to happen, we don't give up. We keep asking. Then we hear a "no," or even more disappointing, no answer. It becomes increasingly apparent that it's not going to happen. The deadline for the payment has passed. The cancer patient we're praying for dies. The day of the decision has come, but still no sense of the Lord's leading. This is where we learn to come with gut-level honesty before the Lord. Prayers of lament sound a lot like complaining or whining. But it's much more appropriate (and effective) to whine and complain with God than with people. We do so respectfully, with submission to Him as the all-knowing, all-wise God. However, He doesn't seem to be bothered by His people who don't take "no" easily. He's okay with us asking, "Why not?"[2]

God's Silence of Love

God also speaks to us in His silence of love. Zephaniah the prophet wrote, "He will be quiet in His love" (3:17, *NASB*). God is silent because words will distract from the love and care God is conveying to us in His quietness.

If you are going through a time in your life when God seems distant, pray for wisdom to interpret the silence. Whether He is silent to test you, judge you or quiet you in His love, He always intends that you put your trust in Him so that He can do a deep work in you. He wants you to know without doubt that you can trust Him.

When God is silent, it doesn't mean that He is absent. King David, on more than one occasion, felt abandoned by God. Despite the silence, David knew he was never out of God's sight. "Where can I go from your Spirit: Where can I flee from your presence? . . . If I settle on the far side of the sea, even there your hand will guide me, your right hand will hold me fast" (Ps. 139:7,9-10).

God promises never to leave us or forsake us (see Heb. 13:5). His silence should be our motivation to hunger and thirst after Him even more. His silence is a reminder of what we are missing. Painful dry spells drive us closer to Him. Remember, during times of drought, roots grow deep into the earth in search of water that will give the tree a better foundation. Times of God's silence prepare us for future storms. It has been well said, "Never forget in the dark what you have learned in the light."

Apply What You've Learned

VERSE TO REMEMBER:

Where can I go from your Spirit? Where can I flee from your presence?
If I go up to the heavens, you are there;
if I make my bed in the depths, you are there.
PSALM 139:7-8

1. How do you hear God through times of suffering?

2. Describe any times when you have heard God's "silence of love."

3. What is a prayer of lament?

Notes

1. Oswald Chambers, *My Utmost for His Highest* (Grand Rapids, MI: Discovery House, 1992).

2. Ron Parrish, *From Duty to Delight* (Lititz, PA: Partnership Publications, 2006), pp. 79-82.

48

Co-laboring with God

A farmer purchases an old rundown abandoned farm with plans to turn it into a thriving enterprise. The fields are grown over with weeds, the farmhouse is falling apart and the fences are collapsing. During his first day of work, the town preacher stops by to bless the man's work, saying, "May you and God work together to make this the farm of your dreams!"

A few months later, the preacher stops by again to call on the farmer. To his surprise, it looks like a completely different place—the farmhouse is completely rebuilt and in excellent condition; there are plenty of cattle and other livestock happily munching on feed in well-fenced pens; and the fields are filled with crops planted in neat rows. "Amazing!" the preacher says. "Look what God and you have accomplished together!"

"Yes, reverend," says the farmer, "but remember what the farm was like when God was working it alone!"[1]

We smile at this story, quite sure that the farmer was mistaken about his overall picture of God. Despite its obvious inaccuracy, however, it has a ring of truth. We are vital participants with God to accomplish His glorious plans here on Earth. We have free will, and along with our independent will we have our own creative ideas as we co-labor with God.

When a farmer plants and tills his field, he is co-laboring with God for the harvest. God cooperates with the farmer, allowing the farmer to use his own (God-given) skills to plant and cultivate. It is a joint effort. We are partners with God, but if it is going to get done, it is up to us, through Christ. He allows us to add our creative expression as He co-labors with us on Earth.

God gave this planet to His people through covenant and partnership. The Bible clearly calls us fellow workers with God: "For we are God's fellow workers . . ." (1 Cor. 3:9); "As God's fellow workers . . ." (2 Cor. 6:1). In his book *The Supernatural Power of a Transformed Mind*, Bill Johnson says that many Christians have a one-dimensional viewpoint of co-laboring:

> They think it's a robotic interplay between themselves and God in which their will is dialed down to zero and his will completely

overtakes their desires and thoughts. . . . But that is exactly the opposite of what the Bible says. In fact, our ideas and desires and dreams have a monumental influence on how God carries out his plan in this world. We are co-laborers, meaning that apart from Christ our work is not complete, and at the same time, amazingly, his work on earth is not complete without us. God looks to you and me as contributors to what he is doing. . . . He is interested in your desires and dreams and has opened up his plan on this planet to your influence.[2]

According to Johnson, the Bible shows us how co-laboring works:

At the creation, God let Adam name all of the animals. Names in those days were more than just cute labels given to distinguish the creatures. Names were assigned according to character. They indicated what kind of being this would be. When God gave Adam the privilege and responsibility of naming all of the animals, he was inviting him to assign character and nature to those creatures he would spend his life with. God created it all; Adam added his creative expression by giving the animals certain natures. That's co-laboring.[3]

Another biblical example of co-laboring includes God's interaction with Moses when God wanted to destroy the wayward Israelites. Moses asked God to reconsider, and God relented because He was interacting with Moses as a friend and heard Moses' plea. We, too, have this friendship with God (see John 15:15). God wants to engage us as a friend as we participate with Him in His work.

It appears that the "normal" method of operation between David and God was for David to do what was in his heart, and for God to promise that He would be with him. This is reflected in Psalm 37:4: "Delight yourself also in the LORD, and he will give you the desires of your heart."

This works two ways: First, He gives us what we long for; but second, He also places a longing in our hearts for things He wants us to have. David, however, never assumed that God's direction for one day would be the same the next day. He listened for the Lord's instructions for each battle he fought.

Philippians 2:13 says it similarly: "For it is God who works in you to will and to act according to his good purpose." God places desires within us to lead us in the way He wants us to go.

So let's get practical. How does this apply to our hearing from God? It is certainly good to pray about everything, but let's not get so super-spiritual that we feel God must give us an angelic visitation to show us which grocery store we should go to, which restaurant to eat at, and whether to go to Wal-Mart, Kmart, Target or Macy's. As we acknowledge Him each day, moment by moment, He directs our steps.

As we learn to practice His presence (as we will learn in the next chapter), I am convinced that the Lord wants us to make many of these decisions in the same way He trusted Adam to name all of the animals. We are co-laboring with God and have the privilege and responsibility to make sound, ordinary decisions in daily life because the Holy Spirit is directing us from within.

God trusts us because we have a friendship with Him. We are no longer operating simply as servants working for Him; we are friends who work with Him. God doesn't have the need to micro-manage our lives! He entrusts us with His power to make decisions as we are changed more and more into His likeness.

Apply What You've Learned

VERSE TO REMEMBER:

For we are God's fellow workers.
1 CORINTHIANS 3:9

1. How can we be partners with God?

2. Describe what it means to you that God calls you "friend."

3. Describe any times when God gave you what you longed for, because that longing had been placed there by God.

Notes

1. "Partners with God." http://www.netfunny.com/rhf/jokes/90q3/godalone.html (accessed September 2007).

2. Bill Johnson, *The Supernatural Power of a Transformed Mind* (Shippensburg, PA: Destiny Image Publishers, 2005), pp. 139-140.

3. Ibid., p. 140.

49

Practicing His Presence

A Christian's body is the temple of the Holy Spirit, and God takes up permanent residence there. He wants you to live daily in His presence. He longs for you to open your spiritual ears to hear Him speak as you walk through your daily life. How is it possible to live minute by minute in the presence of God?

In his book *Just Like Jesus*, Max Lucado wrote that when he realized he could continually be in the presence of God, it revolutionized his life. For years he viewed God as a compassionate boss, and his role as one of a loyal employee. God was as close as a phone call or fax away and encouraged him, but He didn't really go *with* him. Then he read 2 Corinthians 6:1, "We are God's fellow workers."

> Imagine the paradigm shift this truth creates. Rather than report to God, we work with God. . . . We are always in the presence of God. . . . There is never a nonsacred moment! His presence never diminishes. Our awareness of His presence may falter, but the reality of His presence never changes.[1]

The Reality of His Daily Presence

The Lord says, "Be still, and know that I am God" (Ps. 46:10). God wants us to experience His presence and continually maintain a God-consciousness. We can enjoy unceasing communion with God, finding in Him all that we need, all of the time.

"Being still" is a presence of mind, a state of rest in the Lord; it does not necessarily mean finding a solitary place and shutting everything else out, although there are times when this is necessary. A mother of young children does not have the option of having extended times of solitude, but it is possible to experience God's presence in the daily routine of changing dirty diapers and car-pooling the kids to soccer practice.

I believe that practicing the presence of God can take place in the midst of your routine as you learn to tune your spirit to loving the

Lord with your whole heart, soul and mind. When you want to please God in your thoughts, deeds and words, your will becomes united with God's will. This affects your attitude. You love God with no other motive than to love Him and listen for His voice.

Brother Lawrence, a monk from the seventeenth century known for his book *The Practice of the Presence of God*, wrote, "We must know before we can love. In order to know God, we must often think of him. And when we come to love him, we shall then also think of him often, for our heart will be with our treasure." Brother Lawrence described this continuous practice of the presence of God as a "quiet, familiar conversation with him."[2] He said the most effective way he had to communicate with God was to do his ordinary work out of a pure love of God. He thought it to be a serious mistake to think of our prayer time as a different time from any other. He said, "I turn my little omelet in the pan for the love of God."[3]

Intentional Listening

Walking in the loving presence of God every day and making each day one continuous prayer can be compared to the biblical challenge to "pray without ceasing" (1 Thess. 5:17). But how is it possible to fellowship with God continually? Can it become as natural as breathing? I believe it can. But we must learn to listen.

Bible teacher Joyce Meyer told her husband one day that they needed to talk more. It seemed to Joyce that he never wanted to just spend time sitting and talking. Her husband responded by saying, "Joyce, we don't talk; *you* talk and I listen."

Joyce confirms, "He was right, I needed to change if I expected him to want to fellowship with me. I also discovered I was doing the same thing with God; I talked and expected God to listen. I complained that I never heard from God, but the truth is I never listened."[4]

This is a good lesson for all of us. For most, listening is an ability that must be developed by practice. If you are a born talker, you never had to work hard at making conversation; but you may have had to make an effort to listen intentionally.

My wife, LaVerne, who has learned over the years the importance of communing with God and having a real love relationship with our Father in heaven, describes it like this:

We as a church are engaged to Jesus, the Bridegroom who is coming back for us—the Bride. What do engaged couples do to have an effective relationship? They spend time together, not just talking, but listening to each other's heart, sharing each other's dreams. As they listen and talk together, they understand each other. If they just talk and do not listen, they have an ineffective relationship. So it is in our relationship with Jesus.

It is Jesus' desire that we listen to Him and commune with Him. When the Word of God is in us, we understand and know who God is. We understand that He wants to speak to us. The Word of God is spirit and life within us. As we drive down the road, as we wash dishes, as we sit at our desk, we are aware of His presence and are willing to listen to that "still, small voice" based on the Word of God, because the Word of God is in us. God desires to speak to us all day long. It is up to us to listen to Him.

Growing and Hearing Go Hand in Hand

According to Hebrews 5:11-14, sometimes our hearing becomes dulled because we are not listening to or obeying the truth we already know. Paul expressed his disappointment with the Hebrew Christians because they had not grown up spiritually and learned to hear and obey God's voice.

> Though by this time you ought to be teachers, you need someone to teach you the elementary truths of God's word all over again. You need milk, not solid food! Anyone who lives on milk, being still an infant, is not acquainted with the teaching about righteousness. But solid food is for the mature, who by constant use have trained themselves to distinguish good from evil (Heb. 5:12-14).

Babies are not ready for solid food. They need to grow first. As spiritual babies grow and mature, they eventually learn to hear and obey God's voice. The Lord does not reveal everything to baby Christians at once; He explains things to them as they are able to understand. If they obey the truth they have, the Lord will be able to reveal new truths He wants them to know.

God will tell us the way to go, but then we have to do the walking, one step of obedience at a time. The Bible says, "The steps of a good man are ordered by the LORD, and He delights in his way. Though he fall, he shall not be utterly cast down; for the LORD upholds him with His hand" (Ps. 37:23-24, *NKJV*). Start right where you are and learn to enjoy practicing His presence in simple faith.

Don't be afraid to make mistakes. By faith, get up and start again. Life is like an American football game. Every time there is a play, the quarterback gets his team into a huddle and they come up with a new play: it is all part of a larger game plan. God gathers us into His huddle and gives us a new plan for the next steps in our game of life.

Jesus gave His life for us on the cross 2,000 years ago. He paid the price for us to experience a loving relationship with our heavenly Father. Practicing His presence each day is about nurturing a love-filled relationship with Him and listening to His voice, minute by minute!

Apply What You've Learned

VERSE TO REMEMBER:

Be still and know that I am God.
PSALM 46:10

1. How can you make each day one continuous prayer?

2. How will practicing God's presence as described in this chapter help you hear God's voice?

3. What are some practical ways you plan to practice God's presence in your daily routine of life?

Notes
1. Max Lucado, *Just Like Jesus* (Nashville, TN: Word Publishing, 1998), p. 59.
2. Brother Lawrence, *The Practice of the Presence of God* (New Kensington, PA: Whitaker House, 1982), pp. 49, 80.
3. Ibid., pp. 24, 80.
4. Joyce Meyer, *How to Hear from God* (New York: Time Warner Book Group, 2003), p. 15.

Watching What the Father Is Doing

"Jesus gave them this answer: 'I tell you the truth, the Son can do nothing by himself; he can do only what he sees his Father doing, because whatever the Father does the Son also does'" (John 5:19).

Sometimes we "hear" with our eyes. For example, we communicate to our children by the way we model our life. They hear us speak by how we live. Our God does the same. He often speaks to us by what we see Him doing among us. We hear Him speak by recognizing what He is doing—and joining Him. God is working continually in and through our life, and He wants us to link with Him in that work.

We must be careful not to assume that God will speak to us in one certain way. By now, you should realize that He may be speaking to you through any of the 50 ways outlined in this book, plus hundreds of other ways. We simply need to look around us to see how He is working and learn to recognize the activity of God.

The prophet Habakkuk once said, "I will look to see what he will say to me" (Hab. 2:1). Many times, that which God is saying to us is right in front of us! A husband may be relaxing and feel impressed to help his wife with some of the maintenance around the house. He should not be too quick to rebuke that thought! It is probably the Lord speaking to him. A teenager listening to her favorite CD or talking to one of her friends on the telephone may hear a voice within telling her to clean her room. It is probably God speaking!

I know that if LaVerne is overwhelmed with a busy schedule and needs a break, I don't need an angelic visitation before I am motivated to handle a task so that she can rest, or before I simply encourage her to sleep in. Because I know God's character and can see Him at work in my wife's life, I understand that He would want to speak rest to her soul.

When we want to give our opinion or counsel to someone the Lord has placed in our lives, we should keep our spiritual eyes open—

the Father is always doing something, and we can easily miss it. We must find out what He is saying to them.

When I pray with people who are going through deep waters, often I literally keep my eyes open to see what the Father is doing as I pray. If they begin to get emotional and cry, this may change the way I am praying, because I am following what I see the Father doing in the person's life.

In his book *Experiencing God*, Henry Blackaby describes a time when his church sensed that God was leading them to reach out to a college campus. For two years they held Bible studies in the dorms, with no results. Pastor Blackaby finally pulled the church's students aside and said, "This week I want you to go to the campus and watch to see where God is working, and join him." He explained further, "No one will ask after spiritual matters unless God is at work in his life. When you see someone seeking God or asking about spiritual matters, you are seeing God at work. If someone starts asking you spiritual questions, whatever else you have planned, don't do it. Cancel what you are doing. Go with that individual and look to see what God is doing there."

On Wednesday, one of the girls reported, "Oh, Pastor, a girl who has been in classes with me for two years came to me after class today. She said, 'I think you might be a Christian. I need to talk to you.' I remembered what you said. I had a class, but I missed it. We went to the cafeteria to talk. She said, 'Eleven of us girls have been studying the Bible, and none of us are Christians. Do you know somebody who can lead us in a Bible study?' As a result of that contact, we started three Bible study groups in the women's dorms and two in the men's dorm. For two years we tried to do something for God and failed. For three days we looked to see where God was working and joined him. What a difference that made!"[1]

I just returned today from a trip to India. The new church where I was ministering was filled with young people from the local college campuses, who came from many different nations. It was easy to see what the Father in heaven is saying to the leaders of this church. He is calling them to reach a younger generation, many from the college campuses from many different nations and train them to take the gospel to their own nations. It would be silly for these leaders to feel that they should abandon this vital ministry outreach in order to reach senior citizens. The Lord is working among international students in their church. As they observe what the Father is doing, they can hear His voice guiding their ministry.

We learn to hear the voice of the Lord through practice and obedience. Sometimes we may feel discouraged trying to discern what is the Lord's voice and what are other voices vying for our attention; but as we continue to listen to the voice of our Shepherd, we will learn the difference.

We have to be willing to trust God and have faith in Him even when we do not understand His ways. Sometimes we do not know the meaning of what God says until we look back later in life. Even if God's thoughts surpass ours, and we do not always understand His ways, God wants us to get to know His ways! That's why we should intentionally listen for His voice and adjust our lives to Him in obedience to that voice.

Years ago, we were at a shopping mall with two young children. In one split second our then four-year-old daughter was missing from view. I instantly called out her name. Thankfully, she quickly responded to the voice of her father. I was so relieved to see her! Our heavenly Father longs for His children to heed His voice.

Lord, teach us to hear Your voice and obey it.

Apply What You've Learned

VERSE TO REMEMBER:

Jesus gave them this answer: "I tell you the truth, the Son can do nothing by himself; he can do only what he sees his Father doing, because whatever the Father does the Son also does."
JOHN 5:19

1. Describe a time when God was speaking something that was right in front of you.

2. Name two basic things we need to do to learn to hear the voice of the Lord.

3. What do you hear and see God doing in you today, and how can you join Him in His work?

Note
1. Henry T. Blackaby and Claude V. King, *Experiencing God* (Nashville, TN: LifeWay Press, 1990), p. 26.

Learning to Listen

If there is one thing I have learned over the years, it is that God is a God of surprises. We can never limit God in any way, including the way He will speak to us. He created us to communicate with Him and He longs for the times when we speak with Him and listen to His voice. What we have explored in this book is that while we can expect God to speak, He might speak in unexpected ways.

It would be easy if we could just dial a number on a spiritual cell phone and hear the reassuring voice of God answering, "Hello, this is God speaking!" In reality, He is speaking to us every day in ways we may often miss. The Bible says, "For God does speak—now one way, now another—though man may not perceive it" (Job 33:14).

The Bible gives us many clues to hearing God's voice. Our ears must be tuned to hear Him. The Lord has an enormous range of options for speaking to us. He may use the inner witness of the Holy Spirit, His Word, prayer, circumstances or other people. The Lord may speak to us in dreams, visions or even by His audible voice; however, don't expect God's audible voice to be the common way He will speak! God's voice often blends into a melodic harmony to which we have to tune in.

Jesus promised that if we listen to Him closely, we will receive more and more from Him. He said, "Be careful what you are hearing. The measure you give will be the measure that comes back to you, and more will be given to you who hear" (Mark 4:24, *AMP*).

When we take the time to listen carefully, we can know the difference between His voice and voices that do not match the character of God, His nature and the history of how He has led others before us. Jesus urges us to learn to listen like sheep: "They will never follow a stranger, but will run away from him because they do not know the voice of strangers or recognize their call" (John 10:5, *AMP*).

But the truth is, even when we diligently seek God for an answer, we sometimes find ourselves struggling to hear. We really want to do what the Lord wants us to do. We know that we serve a living God who speaks to us, and yet we struggle with the fact that we do not hear Him as clearly as we would like.

Other times we think we have heard the Lord's voice and respond to it, only to find that we were wrong. Instead of pressing in to find out why we "missed it," we hesitate to step out in faith the next time.

That's why I wrote this book. I want you to discover that God wants to speak to you even more than you desire to hear from Him, and He has many different ways to communicate with you. We cannot put Him in a box.

His voice becomes familiar to us as we develop a relationship with Him. If you do not have a relationship with God through Jesus Christ, the Bible, which is God's inspired and true word, makes it clear that Jesus is Truth. To be a Christian means that you establish your life on the truth of Jesus. Jesus Himself said, "I am the way and the truth and the life. No one comes to the Father except through me" (John 14:6). The Bible says that when we accept Jesus as our Lord and Savior, we are given a deposit of the Holy Spirit as a promise of what is yet to come (see 2 Cor. 5:5). With the presence of the Holy Spirit within, we receive the help we need to pray and discern what our heavenly Father is saying to us (see 1 Cor. 2:11).

Although we have considered more than 50 different ways the Lord speaks to us in this book, these are not the only ways He may choose to communicate. God is sovereign. He speaks in different ways at different times. Our faith must always be in God and not in a certain method.

Among the myriad ways God speaks, we may not consider some to be particularly spiritual. For example, we learned that God can speak through common sense. If you want to buy a new house and cannot afford it, God is probably telling you to wait until He provides the money for you.

I have found that even those who have experienced divine intervention or amazing angelic visitations acknowledge that most often the Lord speaks to them through the Word of God, the peace of God, circumstances, His still small voice, other Christians and through commonsense wisdom.

Even with that said, our God is so infinitely amazing, wise and creative that He does not limit Himself to speaking in the same way all of the time. God thinks outside the box! He is a little unpredictable, not unlike Aslan the lion in *The Chronicles of Narnia*: "One day you'll see him and another you won't. He doesn't like being tied down—and of course he has other countries to attend to. It's quite all right. He'll often drop in. Only you mustn't press him. He's wild, you know. Not like a tame lion."[1]

If you want to hear from God, you must trust Him even if there is no "one safe method" or formula to hear from Him. Allow God to surprise you! Trust Him to speak to you. Cultivate your friendship with Him. You are in a lifetime walk with the Creator of the universe, and hearing His voice is a skill to be learned over time.

My prayer for you is that you will experience the Lord's presence and hear His voice in a whole new dimension as you continue your lifetime walk with Jesus. Let's together fulfill the Lord's purpose for our lives as we look forward to His return. May the Lord bless you richly as you listen to Him speak to you and experience the joy of obeying His voice.

Your fellow servant in Christ,

Larry Kreider

Note
1. C. S. Lewis, *The Chronicles of Narnia* (New York: Macmillan Publishing Company, 1950), p. 194.

Author Contact

Larry Kreider is the founder and International Director of DOVE Christian Fellowship International (DCFI), an international family of churches that has successfully used the New Testament strategy of building the Church with small groups for more than 25 years. DOVE, an acronym for "Declaring Our Victory Emmanuel," started as a youth ministry in the late 1970s that targeted unchurched youth in south-central Pennsylvania. DCFI grew out of the ensuing need for a flexible New Testament-style church (new wineskin) that could assist these new believers (new wine). Today, the DCFI family consists of cell-based congregations and house churches that network throughout the United States, Central and South America, the Caribbean, Canada, Europe, Africa, Asia and the South Pacific.

Contact Information for Seminars and Speaking Engagements

Larry Kreider, International Director
DOVE Christian Fellowship International
11 Toll Gate Road
Lititz, Pennsylvania 17543
Telephone: 717-627-1996
Fax: 717-627-4004

www.dcfi.org
LarryK@dcfi.org

Larry would like to hear your story describing the ways you have heard God's voice and how your prayers have been answered. Larry is planning to write more books on hearing the voice of God and answered prayer, and your story may be included in future books. Please email your story to yourstory@dcfi.org.

Resources from DCFI
(www.dcfi.org)

Books

Building Your Personal House of Prayer
Larry Kreider
Destiny Image Publishers, $15.99
ISBN: 076-8-42662-6
With the unique "house plan" developed in this book,
each room in your house corresponding to a part of the Lord's
Prayer, your prayer life is destined to go from duty to joy!
Includes a helpful Daily Prayer Guide.

The Biblical Role of Elders for Today's Church
Larry Kreider, Ron Myer, Steve Prokopchak and Brian Sauder
House to House Publications, $12.99
ISBN: 978-1-886973-62-6
New Testament principles for equipping church leadership
teams: Why leadership is needed, what their qualifications and
responsibilities are, how they should be chosen, how elders
function as spiritual fathers and mothers, how they are to
make decisions, resolve conflicts, and more.

Biblical Foundation Series
Larry Kreider
House to House Publications
$4.99 each, 12-book set $39
ISBN: 978-1-886973-18-3
This series covers basic Christian doctrine. Practical illustrations
accompany the easy-to-understand format. Use for small-group
teachings (48 in all), a mentoring relationship or as a daily
devotional. Series includes:

1. *Knowing Jesus Christ as Lord*
2. *The New Way of Living*
3. *New Testament Baptisms*
4. *Building for Eternity*
5. *Living in the Grace of God*
6. *Freedom from the Curse*
7. *Learning to Fellowship with God*
8. *What Is the Church?*
9. *Authority and Accountability*
10. *God's Perspective on Finances*
11. *Called to Minister*
12. *The Great Commission*

House to House
Larry Kreider
House to House Publications, $8.95
ISBN: 978-1-880828-81-6
How God called a small fellowship to become a house-to-house
movement. DOVE Christian Fellowship International has grown
into a family of cell-based churches and house churches networking
throughout the world. This book is also a training handbook for
small-group leaders.

Helping You Build Cell Churches Manual
Compiled by Brian Sauder and Larry Kreider
House to House Publications, $19.95
ISBN: 978-1-886973-38-1
A complete biblical blueprint for cells, this manual covers 51 topics
for training to build cell churches from the ground up.
Includes study and discussion questions. Use for training cell
leaders or for personal study.

Training

Church Planting and Leadership (Live or Video School)
Larry Kreider and others
Prepare now for a lifetime of ministry and service to others.
The purpose of this school is to train the leaders our world is
desperately looking for. We provide practical information as well as
Holy Spirit empowered impartation and activation. Be transformed
and prepared for a lifetime of ministry and service to others. If you
know where you are called to serve—church, small group, business,
public service, marketplace—or you simply want to grow in your
leadership ability, our goal is to help you build a biblical foundation
to be led by the Holy Spirit and pursue your God-given dreams.
For a complete list of classes and venues, visit www.dcfi.org.

School of Global Transformation
(seven-month residential, discipleship school)
Be equipped for a lifetime of service in the church, marketplace
and beyond! The School of Global Transformation is a seven-
month, residential, discipleship school that runs September through
March. Take seven months to satisfy your hunger for more of God.
Experience His love in a deeper way than you ever dreamed possible.
He has a distinctive plan and purpose for your life. We are committed to helping students discover their destiny in Him and prepare
them to transform the world around them.
For details, visit www.dcfi.org.

Seminars

One-day seminars with Larry Kreider and other DOVE Christian
Fellowship International authors and leaders. Topics include:

How to Fulfill Your Calling as a Spiritual Father/Mother
How to Build Healthy Leadership Teams
How to Hear God
Called Together Couples Mentoring
How to Build Small Groups (Basics)
How to Grow Small Groups (Advanced)

Counseling Basics
Effective Fivefold Ministry Made Practical
Starting House Churches
Planting Churches Made Practical
How to Live in Kingdom Prosperity

For more information about DCFI seminars,
call 800-848-5892
or email seminars@dcfi.org.

More from
Larry Kreider

Authentic Spiritual Mentoring
Nurturing Younger Believers
Toward Spiritual Maturity
Larry Kreider
ISBN 978.08307.44138

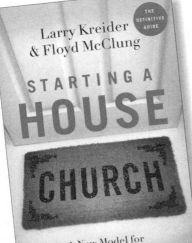

Starting a House Church
A New Model for
Living Out Your Faith
Larry Kreider and Floyd McClung
ISBN 978.08307.43650